More Praise for *Whom Shall I Fear?*

Rosalind Hughes recognizes fear as a given in human experience. Instead of prescribing an answer, she stirs scripture, history, current events (sometimes tragic), doors, locks, guns, and "security systems" into a stew and then poses questions to help readers come to their own conclusions. Faith is the opposite of binding fear. Faith liberates. But true faith has to be found inside. This book is a first-rate map to the faith already there in every heart.

—The Rt. Rev. Dan Edwards
National Chair of Episcopal Peace Fellowship
and Retired Bishop of the Episcopal Diocese of Nevada

This is a necessary book. The Rev. Hughes has written a powerful book asking critical questions from a perspective of shared gospel values. With references from scripture and stories from her personal and pastoral experience, we examine what it means to be a Christian community in violent times. I'm eager to read this again with compassionate others to consider how we can open our hearts even when our fears might cause us to want to lock our doors.

—The Rev. Kristine Eggert
Cofounder and Executive Director,
God Before Guns

D1300236

In a society that continues to arm itself at a fearful rate, the Rev. Rosalind Hughes helps us explore what it might mean to put on the armor of light. With exceptional scholarly and pastoral ability, she both challenges and emboldens us to a deeper self-examination through the lens of scripture and a pedagogy of humility and vulnerability. *Whom Shall I Fear?* is a timely gift to an uncertain church in an unstable world.

—The Rt. Rev. Mark Hollingsworth Jr.
Bishop of the Episcopal Diocese of Ohio

WHOM
SHALL I
FEAR
?

WHOM SHALL I FEAR ?

URGENT QUESTIONS FOR CHRISTIANS
IN AN AGE OF VIOLENCE

ROSALIND C. HUGHES

UPPER
ROOM BOOKS®
NASHVILLE

Cover design: Lindy Martin, Faceout Studio
Cover imagery: MJgraphics, Shutterstock
Interior design and typesetting: PerfecType | Nashville, TN

Library of Congress Cataloging-in-Publication Data available upon request
ISBN: 978-0-8358-1967-1
Mobi ISBN: 978-0-8358-1968-8
Epub ISBN: 978-0-8358-1969-5

Printed in the United States of America

CONTENTS

Contents

CHAPTER EIGHT
And a Child Shall Lead Them

CHAPTER NINE
Many Sparrows

PREFACE

The LORD is my light and my salvation;
    whom shall I fear?
The LORD is the stronghold of my life;
    of whom shall I be afraid?
I believe that I shall see the goodness of the LORD
    in the land of the living.
Wait for the LORD;
    be strong, and let your heart take courage;
    wait for the LORD!

                           —PSALM 27:1, 13-14

A community police officer unknowingly planted the seed for this book when he told an assembled group of church leaders, members, and clergy, "You're not going to like this, but in an active shooter situation, you may have to leave behind the people who are too old, too slow, too unable to get out of the way."

It was not said without compassion—quite the opposite. The officer knew that this advice went against every instinct of a caring community, with or without faith. But he was a realist. In an emergency where every second spent getting to safety might be the difference between life and death, there is no time to wait on the weak. From his perspective, we must be prepared to harden our hearts to survive in a world like ours.

This was the first but not the last time that I heard the sound advice of law enforcement agencies, security firms, and first responders rub up against the mandates of the gospel: Love God and love your neighbor as yourself. Your old neighbor. Your infirm neighbor. Your ill-dressed, oddly behaved, visiting neighbor. Your inconvenient neighbor. Your fearful neighbor. Your neighbors with their heads in the sand in denial. Your neighbor the enemy.

I came to understand the problem as one of mission. All sorts of people are eager to mitigate the fear generated by an avalanche of mass shootings in this country. The agencies presenting their solutions and suggestions are driven by motives that might at times overlap but are not at one with the mission of a church, the hope of the gospel.

Hardness of heart, while it may help a tactical officer do his job, is not one of the gifts of the Spirit in Paul's letters to the churches (see 1 Corinthians 12:4-11). Paul ends that chapter by saying "But strive for the greater gifts. And I will show you a still more excellent way" (1 Cor. 12:31). Then he launches into his famous appeal to the power and endurance of love in chapter 13.

This book is not designed to tell a congregation how to keep their church and community safe from harm, crime, or evil intent. There are plenty of agencies, individuals, and programs expertly designed for that purpose. Rather, this is an opportunity to take a step back from the fear, especially fear that is used in marketing solutions for profit, whether that profit be money or power and influence.[1] As Jesus tells us, one cannot faithfully and simultaneously serve both God and mammon (see Matthew 6:24, KJV).

This book encourages its readers to examine the gospel for cues about where God is working in all of this chaos, on what the call of Christ is to a given community in the face of fear, and how, even while developing sensible security solutions, to remain faithful to the gospel of love when bad news abounds around us.

It asks difficult questions about how to be a Christian, walking in the Way of the Cross, while we are surrounded by armed guards and a prodigious number of guns. A 2018 Small Arms Survey puts the number of guns in civilian hands in the United States at 393.3 million, the highest rate of private gun ownership in the world.[2]

This book asks if locking the doors of worship is tantamount to storing up treasures where thieves may break in and moths devour. It asks what we are teaching our children about the fear of God and the message of the angels, "Do not be afraid," when they come to church weary from a week of lockdown drills and anxious adult vigilance. It asks the question posed by the psalmist and the hymn-writer: "The LORD is my light and my salvation; whom shall I fear?" (Ps. 27:1).

Above all, it is guided by scripture, by an exploration of the stories of our spiritual ancestors, who themselves faced danger, difficulties, and God. Inspired by their deliberations, decisions, and hard reckoning, this book seeks to live out the advice of the apostle Paul:

> Do not be conformed to this world, but be transformed by the renewing of your minds, so that you may discern what is the will of God—what is good and acceptable and perfect.
>
> —ROMANS 12:2

The Church's One Foundation

Come to him, a living stone, though rejected by
mortals yet chosen and precious in God's sight, and
like living stones, let yourselves be built into a spiritual house, to be a holy priesthood, to offer spiritual
sacrifices acceptable to God through Jesus Christ.
For it stands in scripture:

> "See, I am laying in Zion a stone,
> a cornerstone chosen and precious;
> and whoever believes in him will not be put to
> shame."

—1 PETER 2:4-6

What is the church, and what is its mission? Is the church a collective, a community, or a cult? Is it a "hospital for sinners"[3] or
the dining room of saints? Is it a sanctuary from the world or a
sacrifice for it? Is its first commission the Great Commission of
Matthew 28:19: "Go therefore and make disciples of all nations,
baptizing them in the name of the Father and of the Son and of
the Holy Spirit"? Is it to keep and to profess the great commandments: "You shall love the Lord your God with all your heart,
and with all your soul, and with all your strength, and with
all your mind; and your neighbor as yourself" (Luke 10:27)?
Does the church, like the apostle Paul, try to be "all things to
all people" that it may "by all means save some" (1 Cor. 9:22)?

My denomination, the Episcopal Church, answers the question this way in the Catechism included at the back of the Book
of Common Prayer:

Q. What is the Church?

A. The Church is the community of the New
   Covenant.

Q. What is the mission of the Church?

A. The mission of the Church is to restore all
   people to unity with God and each other in
   Christ.

Q. How does the Church pursue its mission?

A. The Church pursues its mission as it prays and
   worships, proclaims the Gospel, and promotes
   justice, peace, and love.

Q. Through whom does the Church carry out its
   mission?

A. The Church carries out its mission through the
   ministry of all its members.[4]

• Does your church have a motto or mission statement?
  What is it? What scriptural references does it draw upon?

• What does it say about the way the church views itself?

• What does it say about the church's responsibility to the
  gospel?

• What does it say about the church's responsibility to the
  world?

• Where are the areas of friction or tension between those
  responsibilities?

• Is it possible for the church to be "all things to all people"?

I pray that you may have the power to comprehend, with all the saints, what is the breadth and length and height and depth, and to know the love of Christ that surpasses knowledge, so that you may be filled with all the fullness of God.

Now to him who by the power at work within us is able to accomplish abundantly far more than all we can ask or imagine, to him be glory in the church and in Christ Jesus to all generations, forever and ever. Amen.

—Ephesians 3:18-21

INTRODUCTION

Whom Shall I Fear?

Happy is the one who is never without fear,
but one who is hard-hearted will fall into calamity.
                                              —PROVERBS 28:14

The fear of the LORD is hatred of evil.
                                              —PROVERBS 8:13

There is no fear in love, but perfect love casts out fear.
                                              —I JOHN 4:18

In *Following Jesus in a Culture of Fear*, Scott Bader-Saye muses on the angels' standard greeting, "Do not be afraid." He used to think that they were apologizing for the understandably terrifying effect that had on those they visited, but he came to believe that they were instead trying to set aside the effects of fear. Startled and terrified people could well have a hard time comprehending the words of God that the angels were sent to impart.[1]

Elijah would no doubt support such a reading. In fear for his life and without hope or strength, he fled into the wilderness. An angel came to him in a dream—perhaps so as not to frighten him in his fragile state—providing sustenance and sending him to the very mountain where Moses had once seen the glory of the Lord pass before him (see 1 Kings 19:1-9; Exodus 33:21-23).

As Elijah sheltered in place, the earth shook, and the wind shattered, and fire ran riot. Yet the Lord was not in the fearful things but in the sheer silence, the utter and absolute calm that followed the storm.

God recognized Elijah's fear and indulged it, making the mountains quake along with his terrified body; but ultimately the word of God was not to be found within the fear but beyond it. When all was calm and terror exhausted, God returned to Elijah and said, "Now, let's try this again." (1 Kings 19:9-13, AP). This time, Elijah was ready to listen.

C. S. Lewis began his pseudonymous work, *A Grief Observed*, with the observation that grief presents itself in a manner akin to fear, with the same quivering, physical sensations.[2] Countless others have observed the phenomenon of love that seems to breed butterflies in the lover's body. Biblically speaking, the love and fear of God are intimately related.[3]

> Hear, O Israel: The LORD is our God, the LORD alone. You shall love the LORD your God with all your heart, and with all your soul, and with all your might. . . . The LORD your God you shall fear.
> —DEUTERONOMY 6:4-5,13

Is it possible to love our neighbors as well as we love ourselves while shrinking in fear from them, or locking our doors for fear they might come among us, or visibly arming ourselves against them?

———

"Be Perfect"

[Jesus said,] "Be perfect, therefore, as your heavenly Father is perfect."

—MATTHEW 5:48

Some Pharisees came, and to test [Jesus] they asked, "Is it lawful for a man to divorce his wife?" He answered them, "What did Moses command you?" They said, "Moses allowed a man to write a certificate of dismissal and to divorce her." But Jesus said to them, "Because of your hardness of heart he wrote this commandment for you."

—MARK 10:2-5

This question of the Pharisees regarding divorce, along with the rest of this whole challenging episode, was the portion of the Gospel appointed by the lectionary for my first Sunday in my new parish.

In the church that I serve as priest, marriage is considered so important and weighty a gift and a blessing that I have permission to solemnize the matrimony of committed couples of any gender and sexual orientation, as long as they share the understanding of mutuality, faithfulness, and perseverance laid out by church canons. I also celebrate second and third marriages, with the permission of my bishop.

Nevertheless, when faced with Jesus' stern words and a new congregation on a bright Sunday morning, I quailed.

"Let's talk about this one when we have had a chance to get to know one another a little better," I suggested, and preached on another lesson of the day, after some nervous chuckling from my new flock.

Different denominations, congregations, and families have different views of these verses, but each has had to set them against the continuing reality of the world of human relationships.

I rather doubt that Jesus was addressing personally those people who have chosen divorce as a way forward or have experienced it unchosen when he spoke of hardened hearts. Rather, I think that he was pointing out that the world in which we live and move and have our being can be hard-hearted. Love is not always true or well-informed, vows are not always gentle, and promises are not always perfect in their making or their keeping. He who came to bring release to the captive recognized that sometimes our own relationships become a prison in this fallen world with its fallout of sin and that we sometimes repent of them.

What if the same is true of other promises and aspirations to enduring relationships?

One church may, with reluctance and regret, find that its promise that "all are welcome" is broken by the incursion of an unwelcome, evil-intentioned visitor.

Another might repent of its hasty union with partners who, on reflection, do not share its values and might even harm its mission.

> As he was setting out on a journey, a man ran up and knelt before him, and asked him, "Good Teacher, what must I do to inherit eternal life?" Jesus said to him, "Why do you call me good? No one is good but God alone. You know the commandments:

'You shall not murder; You shall not commit adul-
tery; You shall not steal; You shall not bear false witness; You shall not defraud; Honor your father and
mother.'" He said to him, "Teacher, I have kept all
these since my youth." Jesus, looking at him, loved
him and said, "You lack one thing; go, sell what you
own, and give the money to the poor, and you will
have treasure in heaven; then come, follow me."

—MARK 10:17-21

Jesus is uncompromising in his words to the Pharisees (partly,
no doubt, because of the tone they used with him) and with this
rich man. But how many of us have followed his instruction to
sell all that we own for the sake of the poor? We read the Gospels
and the Bible to find the kingdom of heaven, the will of God for
the world, knowing that we are not yet tempted to follow it perfectly. Yet Jesus looked upon the man and loved him.

Jesus is uncompromising but not unforgiving. He has empa-
thy for the tender-hearted—who live like aliens in a hard-hearted
world—and even for those whose hearts are a little scabby. His
resurrected body carries in its side an open and a bleeding heart.

And like love newly awakened, Jesus' resurrection always
reminds us of the possibility of a new creation.

A new heart I will give you, and a new spirit I will
put within you; and I will remove from your body
the heart of stone and give you a heart of flesh.

—EZEKIEL 36:26

The chapters that follow will call into question our ability to resist being conformed to the world, even as we proclaim a transformative gospel (see Romans 12:2). The first chapter will engage with a guided meditation about locked doors. The dilemma in my own church is not about whether to lock our doors during worship but during the hospitality hour, when the greeters are away from their stations and strangers wander the halls looking for help. We are uncomfortable when we come upon them unexpectedly; yet we call it the *hospitality hour*. We recognize the irony.

The second chapter revisits the ethical dilemma of how to live faithfully in an unfaithful world. It sets the scene for chapter 3, which engages head-on the question of armed security in a church setting.

Chapters four through six consider our duty of hospitality, not only to angels who might visit our unaware congregations but also to our mortal neighbors. It looks beyond the concern for our own safety to the welfare and well-being of those who surround us and those who pass us by.

The tragic phenomenon of school shootings has caused us all to think differently and more often about the vulnerabilities of public spaces and public worship. In chapters seven and eight, some survivors of similar tragedy talk about how their faith has helped them and their communities.

Finally, we bring our thoughts and prayers to bear on what we can do not only for ourselves but also to transform the world around us, to facilitate that reconciliation to God and to one another that Christ himself prays for us.

- Which parts of the gospel are you uncomfortable discussing in your congregation?

- When the real talk, the high call of the gospel rubs up against the hard-hearted realities of the world, where do you find your compromise? Give an example.
- How might the promises of deep understanding, forgiveness, and reconciliation, even resurrection, provoke and encourage you to live out the gospel boldly?

———

"I am not asking you to take them out of the world, but I ask you to protect them from the evil one. They do not belong to the world, just as I do not belong to the world. Sanctify them in the truth; your word is truth. As you have sent me into the world, so I have sent them into the world. And for their sakes I sanctify myself, so that they also may be sanctified in truth.

"I ask not only on behalf of these, but also on behalf of those who will believe in me through their word."

—JOHN 17:15-20

ONE

Behold, I Stand at the Door and Knock

He shatters the doors of bronze,
and cuts in two the bars of iron.

—PSALM 107:16

When it was evening on that day, the first day of the week, and the doors of the house where the disciples had met were locked for fear of the Jews, Jesus came and stood among them and said, "Peace be with you."

—JOHN 20:19

I know your works. Look, I have set before you an open door, which no one is able to shut. I know that you have but little power, and yet you have kept my word and have not denied my name.

—REVELATION 3:8

This chapter looks at locked and open doors through biblical, spiritual, and practical lenses and asks a congregation to imagine the gospel that their very doors proclaim to those who pass through or pass by.

A quick study of locked doors in the Bible might seem to give them a mixed review.

Sometimes, they are a sign of safety, as in Psalm 147:12-13, in which God, the Lord of Zion strengthens the bars of the gates and blesses the children within; or when God shuts Noah, his family, and the representatives of all flesh into the ark before the Flood.

> Those that entered, male and female of all flesh, went in as God had commanded him; and the LORD shut him in.
>
> —GENESIS 7:16

In both of these cases, the image is of a retreat and hiding place from great danger.

When I was young, I worshiped in a church built in the traditional architectural style of an upside-down boat. The vaulted ceiling brought to mind the seats of oarsmen, and I learned much later that this was purposeful. The name of the place where the people gather—the nave—comes from the same root as *naval, navy: ship.* The church was an ark, a place of refuge, of rescue, of salvation from the storms that assault the world. In the biblical account, God fastens Noah and his family and the animals into the ark for safekeeping until the storm of wrath and death is over.

God later repents of the Flood strategy, establishing a one-sided covenant with the whole of creation that humankind has no power to destroy, and signing it with the rainbow (see Genesis 8:20–9:17). It is an act of self-sacrifice, the decision of the Divine to withhold retaliation, which we see again as the story of our faith continues through the Cross.

In other places in the Bible, locked doors are a sign not of God's providence or protection but of bleak abandonment. Shut-up houses are a sign of God's judgment on the cities of the earth:

The city of chaos is broken down,
    every house is shut up so that no one can enter.
                                            —Isaiah 24:10

Locked doors can also work to the detriment of those locked inside. When David holed up in a walled city, Saul besieged and isolated him by using David's defenses against him.

Now it was told Saul that David had come to Keilah. And Saul said, "God has given him into my hand; for he has shut himself in by entering a town that has gates and bars."
                                            —1 Samuel 23:7

Reading across the sweep of the Bible, we find that the ideal of the age to come is one in which doors are open and gates never need to be shut, by day or by night (see Isaiah 60:11).

In Revelation, the gates of the holy city stand open all day and there is no night.

The city has no need of sun or moon to shine on it, for the glory of God is its light, and its lamp is the Lamb. The nations will walk by its light, and the kings of the earth will bring their glory into it. Its gates will never be shut by day—and there will be no night there. People will bring into it the glory and the honor of the nations.
                                            —Revelation 21:23-26

In the vision, there is no longer any danger or threat that would cause them to be closed; no abomination may enter (see Revelation 21:27). This is not our reality; we do not live without danger. But we do proclaim the vision of the kingdom of heaven close at hand. Whether we choose to lock our doors against danger or open them wide to the grand procession of glory (or whether we decide to find some creative middle way), we need to pay careful heed to Jesus' warnings to the hypocrites:

> "Woe to you, scribes and Pharisees, hypocrites! For you lock people out of the kingdom of heaven. For you do not go in yourselves, and when others are going in, you stop them."
>
> —MATTHEW 23:13

———

Take a few moments to sit with the image of a locked door. You might imagine a door with which you are thoroughly familiar: See yourself turning the key to your house or clicking open your car. You might find an image of the "ideal" of a locked door: a heavy, iron affair with padlocks and bolts, or a sleek, futuristic slider protected by biometrics.

Consider the following questions:
- Who locked the door?
- On which side of the door are you?
- Do you have the key?
- Who is with you?
- Who is on the other side of the door?
- Do you feel safe, shut out, or trapped?
- Who will unlock the door?
- Where is Jesus?

———

I have sat on church steps, in the shade of iron-bolted doors, and wept. I have left my doors unlocked for all the world to come and go. I have suffered some minimal loss. I am not altogether naïve about the need for physical boundaries, or their limitations. My personal experience influences the way I assess the recommendations that security professionals and safety experts offer around locking or not locking church doors. Yours will too. Knowing that, let's turn back to the Bible and look at a couple of scenes that might shift our imagination toward God's vision for our congregations and their doors.

———

The books of Ezra and Nehemiah tell the story of the return after the Babylonian exile of the political and priestly leaders of the people of Israel to Jerusalem, its rebuilding and rededication to the Lord of their ancestors. Once again, the people find themselves a minority among many nations. Chastened by their experience of exile and oppression, they are determined to re-establish themselves as a nation and consecrate themselves to the God of their ancestors and their ancient covenants.

To *consecrate* is to set apart. The people were concerned with purity and with cohesion. While they chose to recognize the kind interventions of King Cyrus as the will of God, even describing him as *messiah*—meaning "anointed"—they were not concerned with converting the surrounding nations (see Isaiah 45:1). It was enough to establish their own borders and keep themselves safe, secure, and sanctified. In contrast to the ideal of Isaiah, before the exile, and Revelation, to which we will return, the gates of the holy city are guarded by day and closed after dark, as though danger is always looking for a way into the city.

We rarely read Ezra and Nehemiah in my church, probably because the situation of the people it addresses is so different from our own. Nehemiah has been cited as a biblical sanction for exclusionary walls by some recent commentators, but that feels to others like an anachronistic reading of Nehemiah's precarious position. We are not surrounded by enemies as Nehemiah's Jerusalem was. We are not a threatened minority. We live in the Western world, in what was once called "Christendom" because of the prevalence of our religion, even to the exclusion or oppression of others along the way.

There are Christian communities that have experienced, and continue to experience, oppression. Historically and predominantly Black churches have a different story to tell than the mainly white churches that are their neighbors, which is to say that the calculation is different for those affected, afflicted, or threatened by the atrocities of white supremacy. But in our current context, for many churches, to claim the tentative status of Ezra-Nehemiah's audience is disingenuous.

For us, an episode in Nehemiah 6 is instructive. The purpose of restoring the city was to house the Temple, the dwelling place of God among God's people. As befits the Divine, Temple service was strictly appointed and observed. Worship was to be the prime directive of the people. But not everyone was on board with the rebuilding of Jerusalem. Nehemiah was right to discern a threat from those opposed to his religion: Even those who pretend to be allies can turn out to be double agents for the devil, and even legitimate dangers can be turned into occasions for sin. At the point of crisis, while enemies from without tried to lure Nehemiah to destruction, agents within attempted to exaggerate the danger to his life in order to tempt him to violate the Temple protocol and defile the very religion he was trying to reestablish (see Nehemiah 6:1-14). Fortunately for all concerned, Nehemiah realized the deception. When they suggested that he lock himself within the Temple, he said,

> "Should a man like me run away? Would a man like me go into the temple to save his life? I will not go in!"
>
> —NEHEMIAH 6:11

Nehemiah was in danger, but he would not value even his own safety over faithfulness to his covenant with God. He was aware of the threats against him, but he would not allow them to replace God as his guide, nor would he allow them to become inflated as idols. Nehemiah's confidence was tested, and he passed.

———

Of course, there is no barrier that can successfully lock out God's grace. The rock rolled against the door of the tomb seems laughable against the witness of Jesus' resurrection. The fear of the apostles, gathered behind locked doors, was no match for the peace-breathing risen Christ (see John 20:19-29).

On Wednesday evenings, when I was at college, a handful of us would gather in the side chapel and celebrate Eucharist under the watchful eye of Holman Hunt's *Light of the World*. In this famous painting, Jesus stands at an ivy-covered door, lantern in hand, and knocks. He is dressed in rich robes, but his feet are bare. The light that he carries is barely a match for the halo of light around his head and his crown. He looks out from the frame with a weary patience. There is no way to know how long he has been standing there, knocking on a door that has, on the outside, on his side, no handle. There is no means of making entry unless someone opens it from the inside.

John of Patmos, directed by "the Amen, the faithful and true witness, the origin of God's creation," writes to the angel of the church at Laodicea:

> "I know your works; you are neither cold nor hot. I wish that you were either cold or hot. So, because you are lukewarm, and neither cold nor hot, I am about to spit you out of my mouth. . . . Listen! I am standing at the door, knocking; if you hear my voice and open the door, I will come in to you and eat with you, and you with me."
> —REVELATION 3:14-16, 20

The decisions that we make to lock or unlock doors cannot be made solely on the basis of our own safety. We have responsibilities, as leaders within and examples to our communities, that extend beyond our walls. During the pandemic crisis, some of us found that our fear of personal illness paled when compared to the fear of causing harm to our communities, of becoming the center of a "super-spreader" event, sowing death and disease among the neighbors we are called to love as ourselves. The question of opening or locking our doors has become more complicated as we assess not only our bodily health but also our unseen influence in the world.

In healthier times, we must soberly and seriously consider any advice that will lock us into our ark where we are secure from the world, and it should be assessed against God's repentance and the sign of the rainbow.

"Look, I have set before you an open door, which no
one is able to shut. I know that you have but little
power, and yet you have kept my word and have not
denied my name."

—REVELATION 3:8

Decisions to lock or unlock doors should be based in the mission of our churches to proclaim the good news of Christ to the
world, making disciples of all nations. We cannot be lukewarm
about the gospel! When we gather, we are told to be prepared to
welcome strangers, angels incognito, who may or may not pass
two or three locked doors to seek out our open-secret entrance
(see Hebrews 13:2; more on this in a later chapter).

If we choose to lock our doors for the security or reassurance
of those on the inside, we should consider any unintended consequences to the physical safety of those gathered should an internal
emergency occur, consulting with the local fire department, for
example, to ensure that escape is still possible and that our fortress
does not become a prison. We should consider the spiritual health
of the community and what we are teaching explicitly or inadver-
tently about who belongs within or without our walls.

As in all things, we should always be ready to give an account
of how our decisions reflect our obedience to the commandments:
Love God, and love your neighbor as yourself.

————

Take another few moments to sit with the image of a door. This
time try to picture one of the doors to your church—the big door,
the secret back door, the office door around the side that delivery
people have such difficulty finding, or the door that nobody uses
and most have forgotten is there.

Consider the following questions:

- Is the door open or closed, locked or unlocked?
- On which side of the door are you?
- Who is with you?
- Who is on the other side of the door?
- Do you have the key?
- Where is Jesus?

———

[Jesus said to them,] "I am the gate. Whoever enters by me will be saved, and will come in and go out and find pasture."

—JOHN 10:9

TWO

Do Not Be Overcome by Evil

Do not repay evil for evil or abuse for abuse; but, on the contrary, repay with a blessing. It is for this that you were called—that you might inherit a blessing.

—1 PETER 3:9

Discipline yourselves, keep alert. Like a roaring lion your adversary the devil prowls around, looking for someone to devour. Resist him, steadfast in your faith.

—1 PETER 5:8-9

Saint Paul writes, "If it is possible, so far as it depends on you, live peaceably with all" (Rom. 12:18). A long tradition of Christian nonviolence, founded by Christ himself, is tested when violence surrounds us or when it seems to. How does the church model the call to resist evil and to follow the Prince of Peace?

It may well be said that Christianity was founded on the most profound act of nonviolence ever witnessed. Not only did Jesus submit himself voluntarily to martyrdom, but he did so when, by his own account, he had more power than any person on earth to end his own suffering, end the wickedness of his tormentors, and bring judgment to the whole situation.

"Do you think that I cannot appeal to my Father, and he will at once send me more than twelve legions of angels?" (Matt. 26:53), Jesus demanded of his arresting officers.

We will return to this scene in the garden of Gethsemane in another chapter.

When Jesus first told his disciples that he was headed down the road that would lead to the Cross, they were, to say the least, uncomfortable. When he "began to teach them that the Son of Man must undergo great suffering . . . and be killed, and after three days rise again" (Mark 8:31), Peter took him by the elbow for a little sidebar to bring him to his senses (see Mark 8:32). But Jesus shrugged him away, saying, "Get behind me, Satan! For you are setting your mind not on divine things but on human things" (Mark 8:33).

———

"You have heard that it was said, 'An eye for an eye and a tooth for a tooth.' But I say to you, Do not resist an evildoer. But if anyone strikes you on the right cheek, turn the other also . . .

"You have heard that it was said, 'You shall love your neighbor and hate your enemy.' But I say to you, Love your enemies and pray for those who persecute you, so that you may be children of your

Father in heaven; for he makes his sun rise on the evil and on the good, and sends rain on the righteous and on the unrighteous."

—MATTHEW 5:38-39, 43-45

It is arguable that we are in more of a quandary today than ever before over how to turn the other cheek and love our enemies. We are formed as much by the ideals of the American way of life, liberty, and the pursuit of happiness as by the scandal of the Cross.

In Christian theology, of course, Jesus' act of self-sacrifice was not a simple martyrdom, as costly and as precious as that might be. Jesus' act of nonviolence defeated the forces of violence that hold sway in the world, even death itself. Furthermore, Jesus' death on the Cross demonstrated something about the nature of God: that God is inclined to self-giving over vengeance, mercy over punishment, restraint over rage, and love over all. The Cross does not, it is important to say, make victimhood glorious but convicts the world of unjust and violent victimization.[1] In dying, Jesus did not succumb to death but undermined the forces that wield it, demonstrating by his resurrection that life is more powerful after all.

———

Early in Moses' life and career, as he began to wrestle with his dual and deeply divided identity—born to slaves and adopted into royalty (see Exodus 1:8–2:10)—he tried to use force to place himself on the side of the oppressed. He found an overseer beating a Hebrew worker to death, and, after looking around to make sure he was not observed, Moses killed the violent man (see Exodus 2:11-12).

If he thought that this act of secret solidarity and revenge would endear him to his fellow Hebrews, Moses was mistaken. The very next day, when he sought to intervene in a fight between his countrymen, they rejected him, making it clear to my imagination that they saw him as still enmeshed in the oppressive regime of the Egyptians and its culture of force, which was expressed in the killing of the cruel man.[2] They were not grateful for his death (see Exodus 2:13-14; Stephen revisits the incident in Acts 7:23-29).

The narrator does not judge Moses' murder one way or the other. Moreover, the rescue of his people from slavery and captivity in later chapters involved plagues and devastating death, both domestic and military. The tenth plague was the death of the first-born children of the people and even the animals of all of Egypt (see Exodus 12:29-30). It caused Pharaoh finally to send the Israelites away, and when his army followed, they suffered further loss of life at the Red Sea (see Exodus 14:5-28). But God did not employ human violence in their defeat but only divine intervention.

In this defining story of the people of God, it is God, the author of life, who writes its outcomes.

———

Take a few moments to sit with these questions:

- Why were his fellow Israelites angry with Moses for killing the Egyptian overseer?
- Was Moses' resort to homicide a symptom of being enmeshed in the systems of oppression in which he had been raised?
- Is there something else Moses might have done when he encountered the violent Egyptian?

- Does the punishment meted out later to Pharaoh's army by God as the Israelites are escaping redeem or convict Moses' earlier, unsuccessful intervention?

———

Beat your plowshares into swords,
    and your pruning hooks into spears;
    let the weakling say, "I am a warrior."
                                            —JOEL 3:10

In days to come . . .
they shall beat their swords into plowshares,
    and their spears into pruning hooks;
nation shall not lift up sword against nation,
    neither shall they learn war any more.
                              —MICAH 4:1, 3; ISAIAH 2:2, 4

Early in the Christian tradition, followers of Jesus considered the imperative of his sacrifice, and many were emboldened to follow a path of nonviolence themselves, embracing martyrdom as a spiritual gift. Ignatius of Antioch, martyred early in the second century CE,[3] begged that no one should attempt to save him from the lions because they would be instruments of God's grace, allowing him to share in the sufferings of Christ. Indeed he offered himself as bread for the Eucharist, the remembrance of Christ's own death and Resurrection:

> I am the wheat of God, and let me be ground by the teeth of the wild beasts, that I may be found the pure bread of Christ.[4]

Justin Martyr, whose name describes his ending, and Irenaeus, whose name means *peace*, both wrote in the second century CE and appealed to the commandment of Jesus to turn the
other cheek when confronted by force (see Matthew 5:39). Each
also appealed to the vision shared by Isaiah and Micah of turning
weapons of war into tools for growing food (see Isaiah 2:4; Micah
4:3).[5] Irenaeus saw this transformation embodied in the wood and
iron of the Cross:

> He has finally displayed the plough, in that the
> wood has been joined on to the iron, and has thus
> cleansed His land; because the Word, having been
> firmly united to flesh, and in its mechanism fixed
> with pins, has reclaimed the savage earth.[6]

It would be difficult to argue that we live in a more dangerous
context than our spiritual forebears. Then, as now, the new order
envisioned by the prophets appeared a long way off. In the meantime we live, whether by design or by human error, in a world
whose ethics are complicated by competing goods and stratifica-
tions of evil.

Today it seems quite possible to proclaim the pacific principles
of the gospel while tacitly accepting a culture of armed security
and widespread gun ownership, just as we who bless the poor and
decry greed as a mortal sin nevertheless live acquiescently within a
capitalist system that depends upon economic competition rather
than compassionate collaboration. It seems beyond our capacity
to be in the world without being of it, without taking to the des-
ert like the hermits of ancient times (and even then, we would
probably demand WiFi). The competitive envy of Cain continues
to kill Abel, and we, forewarned as Abel was not, are tempted to
defend ourselves against our brother (see Genesis 4:1-8).

Jesus taught his disciples to pray, "Rescue us from the evil one" (Matt. 6:13), but to wait on divine intervention takes the patience of a saint.[7] When it comes to resisting evil in the meantime, what license might we take beyond turning the other cheek? What is the acceptable range of behaviors between turning the other cheek and violent resistance or retaliation?

During the Second World War, Dietrich Bonhoeffer reflected on these questions as the Nazi authorities closed in for his arrest. Writing to friends a few months before his arrest and imprisonment,[8] Bonhoeffer laid bare the dilemma of a man caught between the humanity of the Incarnation rendered in the gospel and the inhumanity of the regime he saw at work around him. Various personal and social virtues are considered in turn in Bonhoeffer's essay, and all fail at the final hurdle to confront evil, being paralyzed by comparisons of greater and lesser good, greater and lesser evils.[9] Even obedient "self-sacrifice," he wrote, in a terrible blow to the pure ethic of the Way of the Cross, "could be exploited for evil ends."[10] The only person left standing with integrity is the one whose only hope is in the mercy of God. No human system can instruct us precisely in how to face each hour, Bonhoeffer advised; only a relationship with the living Spirit of God can guide us.[11]

The "myth of redemptive violence," as Walter Wink has described it,[12] is set in a moment of crisis against what we might call the myth of redemptive victimhood, when self-sacrifice supports rather than undermines systems of oppression and outbreaks of deadly violence. The abuse of a theology of redemptive suffering taken to its extreme leads to a suspicion that the God who stands with the oppressed, the murdered, and the martyred somehow acquiesces to oppression, murder, and martyrdom.[13] The sacrificial lamb becomes a sitting duck.

But Jesus' work on the Cross does not affirm the power and authority of those opposed to the life of God.

Kelly Brown Douglas, womanist theologian, Episcopal priest, and seminary dean, has explored violence and victimhood through the lens of American racism and the death of Trayvon Martin. She insists that the meaning of the Crucifixion is found only in the life of the Resurrection. The Resurrection's unequivocal rejection of the ends of the Cross makes clear that God opposes its tormenting means and methods.[14]

Bonhoeffer, in his Christmas 1942 essay, concluded that it might become necessary for a Christian to reach a compromise with their conscience in order to resist evil effectively. He described a bold sinner tolerated and forgiven by a God who understands our most profound moral dilemmas; a God who understands that we are unable to avoid being stained by the evil that abounds in this world, even when we are attempting love.[15]

We are going to make terrible and awful choices that may go against the very grain of our being, Bonhoeffer suggests, and the God who demands our moral courage forgives us that moral injury. Yet others have insisted that to succumb to violence in order to defeat violence is itself a defeat; that when we use the instruments of an enemy against them, we put on their mantle and become the enemies of our own salvation, the pounders of nails instead of the makers of ploughs.[16]

———

Jesus' action on the Cross, in and beyond the tomb, and after the Resurrection was powerful in its nonviolent and perfect resistance to evil. Still, like Moses and Bonhoeffer, we live in systems of corruption that demand our resistance but—by their corrupt and corrupting nature—tempt us to acquiesce to or even to employ the instruments of violence.

The overarching question for churches responding to an era of violence in America is how to overwhelm evil with good and resist evil without making peace with its methods or glorifying innocent suffering. How do we repay abuse with a blessing and continue our work that was called into being by the redemption wrought by Christ's overwhelming, nonviolent, selfless, and life-giving love?

Prayerfully consider the following questions:

- Why do Joel, Micah, and Isaiah offer competing oracles about swords and plowshares?
- What does the Cross teach us about resisting evil?
- What does the Resurrection say about innocent suffering?
- When (or if) we are faced with an overwhelming evil, are our choices diminished, expanded, or confirmed?

Do not repay anyone evil for evil, but take thought for what is noble in the sight of all. If it is possible, so far as it depends on you, live peaceably with all. . . . Do not be overcome by evil, but overcome evil with good.

—ROMANS 12:17-18, 21

THREE

Who Will Heal Malchus's Ear?

Blessed are the poor in spirit, for theirs is the
kingdom of heaven.
Blessed are those who mourn, for they will be
comforted.
Blessed are the meek, for they will inherit the earth.
Blessed are those who hunger and thirst for
righteousness, for they will be filled.
Blessed are the merciful, for they will receive mercy.
Blessed are the pure in heart, for they will see God.
Blessed are the peacemakers, for they will be called
children of God.
Blessed are those who are persecuted for righteousness'
sake, for theirs is the kingdom of heaven.
—MATTHEW 5:3-10

*"At that hour Jesus said to the crowds, 'Have you come out with swords
and clubs to arrest me?'" (Matt. 26:55). Do deadly weapons belong in
the house of God, the home of the body of Christ?*

The legal status of guns in churches—in pockets in the pews or in the holsters of professional or volunteer security teams—varies across states and denominations and bears close and advised study by any church that is considering inviting guns into the sanctuary. The biblical status of a weapon designed long after the original writers had rested their hands likewise calls for careful, prayerful, and humble examination of the relevant texts. In sections of American culture, the gun has taken on weightier symbolism than its materials might suggest. To some, it is a smelted and cast idol; to others, an heirloom. To some, it is a uniform; to others, an accessory. To some, it is a necessary evil. To others, the phrase "necessary evil" flies in the face of the goodness of God's creation. Samuel Colt's revolver was eventually marketed as "the Peacemaker"; this has been heard both as the ironic fulfillment and as a blasphemous appropriation of Jesus' beatitude, "Blessed are the peacemakers, for they will be called children of God" (Matt. 5:9).

———

Being aware of the preconceptions we bring to our Bible study and to our community conversations can be helpful. Consider the following questions. If you are in a group, try to listen for the experience of someone who has a different background and culture than your own.

- What is your relationship with guns?
- Is the gospel relevant to our modern weaponry, unthought of in Jesus' time? Why, or why not?

———

When Jesus was arrested in the garden of Gethsemane, he would not allow blood to be shed on his behalf, even though the blood was not as innocent as his.

All four Gospels tell some version of the story. After his last meal with his beloved friends, Jesus goes out to the valley to pray in a garden that was a favorite haunt of his. The Son of Man wrestles with God like Jacob in the Jabbok (see Genesis 32:22-32) while his disciples doze. Then the armed crowd comes for him, following Judas the betrayer, one of his own who kisses him while others grab him (see Matthew 26:36-56; Mark 14:32-50; Luke 22:39-53; John 18:1-11).

In Mark, Jesus simply speaks past the violence of his followers, as someone severs the ear of a slave of the high priest (see Mark 14:47-48).

In John, the slave has a name—Malchus—and Jesus addresses Peter, whose sword has done the severing: "Put your sword back into its sheath. Am I not to drink the cup that the Father has given me?" (John 18:10-11). He also intercedes with the authorities on behalf of his friends (see John 18:8-9).

Perhaps Matthew is the most pointed in his exposition of the moment, having Jesus say to the swordsman, "Put your sword back into its place; for all who take the sword will perish by the sword" (Matt. 26:52). It is according to Matthew that Jesus asks those coming for him, "Do you not think that I could call down the superior firepower of heaven, if I wanted to?" (Matt. 26:53, AP). But he refuses to escalate the violence.

According to Luke, the disciples actually ask Jesus if they should strike, but they do not wait for an answer (see Luke 22:49-50). Perhaps in the melee, Jesus does not hear the question. But when Jesus hears the slave scream and sees the blood from his

severed ear, he scolds his would-be protectors, " 'No more of this!'
And he touched his ear and healed him" (Luke 22:51).

A modern American might ask, "That's all very well for Jesus
(see reference to superior firepower above). He can make that
choice for himself, but what about his disciples? Don't they have
the right to defend themselves and their loved ones against the
mob coming 'with swords and clubs'?" (See Luke 22:52.)

After all, one might say, it is clear from the temptations of
Christ in the wilderness that intentional helplessness is not much
(if any) better than domination.

> Then the devil took him to the holy city and placed
> him on the pinnacle of the temple, saying to him, "If
> you are the Son of God, throw yourself down; for it
> is written,
>
> > 'He will command his angels concerning you,'
> > and, 'On their hands they will bear you up,
> > so that you will not dash your foot against a
> >   stone.' "
>
> Jesus said to him, "Again it is written, 'Do not put
> the Lord your God to the test.' "
>
> —MATTHEW 4:5-7

One friend whose congregation has become tragically
acquainted with violence urged me, "You have to do whatever it
takes to protect your people."

———

A local nondenominational congregation shared the biblical basis
for their own armed security ministry:

When a strong man, fully armed, guards his castle,
his property is safe. But when one stronger than he
attacks him and overpowers him, he takes away his
armor in which he trusted and divides his plunder.

—LUKE 11:21-22

Jesus, in this epigram, is using the imagery of castles and
keeps to represent spiritual forces under siege and assuring his
followers and critics alike that his spiritual power is superior, as he
has demonstrated in the routing of demons. Yet, as we have seen,
when the question is called by his arrest in the garden, Jesus does
not call down the forces of heaven to defeat his human enemies.
Further questions of property and plunder aside, our situation is
very different, our weaponry is deadlier from a distance, and the
threat that churches are considering is not usually from an armed
and organized group of police and officials, as was the case for
Jesus and his disciples, but from a random, or a not so random,
would-be mass shooter.

Another verse from earlier in Luke 22 is sometimes cited in
defense of arming Christian disciples. Directly before heading out
to the Mount of Olives and the garden,

> [Jesus] said to them, "When I sent you out with-
> out a purse, bag, or sandals, did you lack anything?"
> They said, "No, not a thing." He said to them, "But
> now, the one who has a purse must take it, and like-
> wise a bag. And the one who has no sword must sell
> his cloak and buy one. For I tell you, this scripture
> must be fulfilled in me, 'And he was counted among
> the lawless'; and indeed what is written about me is

being fulfilled." They said, "Lord, look, here are two
swords." He replied, "It is enough."

—LUKE 22:35-38

In almost any discussion of weapons in church, either ban-
ning or employing them, this passage and the tale of Malchus's
ear may be set against one another. But historically, they have
been considered by some church fathers not as opposites, or in
contradiction to one another, but working together to convey the
gospel of Jesus.

In the fourth century, Saint Ambrose of Milan imagined the
whole exchange metaphorically: The sword that the disciples
must carry was the word of life, the word of the gospel, which was
falling upon uncomprehending ears. In that case, Peter was doing
Malchus a favor, removing his false ears so that Jesus could heal
and restore his inner hearing, his deeper understanding, with the
healing ointment of the gospel.[1] Clearly, however, this does not
translate easily to a flesh-and-blood setting of twenty-first-century
armed guards.

In the fifth century, Cyril of Alexandria agreed that the
instruction to buy a sword was not an instruction to the disciples
concerning their self-defense, nor did he think it was related to the
events that were immediately to follow at Gethsemane. Instead,
Cyril counted it as part of Jesus' broader apocalyptic prophecies
about the terrors that would befall the nation a generation after
his crucifixion.[2] Cyril argued that the scene in the garden dem-
onstrates that Christ would have us counter terror with love and
use the spiritual armor later described by Paul in Ephesians to
counter persecutors.[3]

Paul advised his readers in Ephesians 6:10-13 to clothe
themselves in the strength of Christ (whose strength is love and

whose armor is the grace of God, who is mighty in compassion and steadfast in mercy). Put on, then, that strength that you may defeat the forces of evil that prey on fear and conscience alike; the powers and principalities of heaven, earth, and the other place alike. Clothe yourself in the armor of God, that you may keep the faith and stand firm against the evil days:

> Stand therefore, and fasten the belt of truth around your waist, and put on the breastplate of righteousness. As shoes for your feet put on whatever will make you ready to proclaim the gospel of peace. With all of these, take the shield of faith, with which you will be able to quench all the flaming arrows of the evil one. Take the helmet of salvation, and the sword of the Spirit, which is the word of God.
>
> Pray in the Spirit at all times in every prayer and supplication.
>
> —EPHESIANS 6:14-18

Some modern commentators, less willing to spiritualize the whole drama, have reconciled the conflict between Jesus' instruction to his disciples and the severing of Malchus's ear by considering the suggestion of selling one's cloak to purchase a sword, and Jesus' weary response to the disciples' eager presentation of two swords between them all, to be "ironic."[4]

- What does it mean to you to "put on the whole armor of God"?
- Jesus implies that the sword will come at a cost. What would we need to "sell out" in order to purchase the sword?

- What do you make of Jesus' statement "All who take the sword will perish by the sword"?

There is a way of reading the life of Christ that finds it to be suffused by prophetic action that both foreshadows and ushers in the coming kingdom of God. By his words, Jesus both unveils and makes real the will of God. His feeding thousands with a few loaves and fish recalls the providence of God in the wilderness, feeds the people in the moment, and predicts a future of God's abundant new providence, an outpouring of sustaining grace. It is not as though the loaves and fish would ever be enough to feed even one thousand people, but by his provident miracle, Jesus points beyond the fish and bread to the new economy of grace, in which no one should go hungry.

In the beginning, when God created the heavens and the earth, the Creator made sure that there was enough food for every living thing that was created. Through his prophetic action, Jesus both *taught* that there was still more than enough food—if it were distributed among the people generously—and *demonstrated* it via the full stomachs of the flesh-and-blood people before him.

If the final conversation between Jesus and his disciples before his arrest is read as a prophetic drama, then the set-up question, "When I sent you out without a purse, bag, or sandals, did you lack anything?" (Luke 22:35) is like his sly question to Philip in John 6: "'Where are we to buy bread for these people to eat?' He said this to test him, for he himself knew what he was going to do" (John 6:5-6). Jesus breaks open the disciples' reliance on old ways of thinking, whether it is calculating the cost of enough bread for the crowd or calculating how many swords one might need to fight for the coming kingdom of heaven.

"It is enough," Jesus says of the swords and, tacitly, of the bread and fish.

In one of the central sacraments of the Christian church, we break bread while praying our remembrance of Jesus' last evening before his arrest and crucifixion, the dinner table conversation and garden conflict. We rehearse the self-giving, life-giving moments of restraint and release. Who among us will fall asleep while Jesus prays drops of blood under the olive trees; and who among us will take the role of the sword-bearer, severing the moment and suffering rebuke?

In between the offering of a few fish and loaves of bread and the outpouring of new manna—God-multiplied food for the five thousand—Jesus prays his thanksgiving (see John 6:11). In between the ironic acceptance of two swords and the scene in the garden, Jesus prays his anguish (see Luke 22:39-46). The prophetic drama is completed when the disciples, still slow to understand how it is that Jesus will save them and how the giving up of his life will, in fact, bring life to the world, strike with the sword, cueing up Jesus once more for an outpouring of healing mercy, forgiving and saving grace beyond our imagination.

> When those who were around him saw what was coming, they asked, "Lord, should we strike with the sword?" Then one of them struck the slave of the high priest and cut off his right ear. But Jesus said, "No more of this!" And he touched his ear and healed him.
>
> —LUKE 22:49-51

Then Jesus said to him, "Put your sword back into its place; for all who take the sword will perish by the sword." (Matt. 26:52)

The whole episode might have been Jesus pressing this point home one last time: that the life he brings is not paid for by the life of any other.

———

Pastor Charles Eduardos used to call himself "the pistol-packing preacher." He has served as a Marine and as a police officer. He still partners with his old police department as a chaplain and has consulted with the Department of Justice. He is also the pastor of a suburban Lutheran parish.

When we met, because of his old nickname, I thought we would talk about his pistol-packing pulpit. But the conversation took an unexpected turn. Although Pastor Eduardos knows that he is the most qualified person in his congregation to wield a weapon, should evil encroach, he has found the strength and the humility to yield that privilege. It is clear that the decision is weighty and the wrestling by no means done with.

———

I mentioned above the question of the innocence of Malchus's blood. He was counted among those who came out against Jesus to arrest him, seeking to kill him, but he was present as the slave of those who wished to get the Christ out of the way. More than that, he was enslaved to a human system of dominance, ambition, oppression (as seen from both above and below), and of violence, a system into which Caiaphas could speak the unspeakable, "You do not understand that it is better for you to have one man die for the people than to have the whole nation destroyed" (John 11:49-50; 18:14), and be both horribly right and tragically wrong at the same time. Christ, his congregant, was willing; the Resurrection, God's loud "no" to crucifixion, tells another story.

The dramatic irony of Caiaphas's statement had everything to do with the way that violence presents itself to us too often and too easily as a solution to troubles and threats. Malchus was enslaved to the power of its myth, and it continues to seduce us today. Elsewhere, Jesus warned that a person cannot serve two competing interests at once (see Matthew 6:24). The congregation that chooses the sword to defend itself should be abundantly clear whom it is serving and make quite sure that it has not been tempted by the sirens of this world.

Perhaps the question becomes, if the sword is wielded or the gun fired, who will heal Malchus's ear? How will the community continue the merciful and gracious outpouring of God's love and forgiveness, demonstrated by Jesus in the garden, after an act of violence by the followers of Christ?

———

- Is it reasonable, appropriate, or indefensible for Christians to defend worship services that remember the events of the garden and the Cross with tools of deadly force?
- If blood is shed, who will heal Malchus's ear, and how?

———

[Jesus said,] "I say to you that listen, Love your enemies, do good to those who hate you, bless those who curse you, pray for those who abuse you. If anyone strikes you on the cheek, offer the other also; and from anyone who take away your coat do not withhold even your shirt. Give to everyone who begs from you; and if anyone takes away your goods, do not ask for them again. Do to others as you would have them do to you. . . .

"Be merciful, just as your Father is merciful."

—Luke 6:27-31,36

FOUR

Hospitality Is Not Only
for Angels

The LORD your God is God of gods and Lord of lords, the great God, mighty and awesome, who is not partial and takes no bribe, who executes justice for the orphan and the widow, and who loves the strangers, providing them food and clothing. You shall also love the stranger, for you were strangers in the land of Egypt.

—DEUTERONOMY 10:17-19

Pursue peace with everyone, and the holiness without which no one will see the Lord.

—HEBREWS 12:14

Let mutual love continue. Do not neglect to show hospitality to strangers, for by doing that some have entertained angels without knowing it.

—HEBREWS 13:1-2

The balance between hospitality to our own congregation and to the visiting stranger can be delicate. How can a church be genuinely and lovingly welcoming, offering sanctuary to those who need it the most?

Entertaining angels without knowing it might actually be for the best. When they make themselves known, angels can wreak havoc.

The angels who visited Abraham under the oaks of Mamre gave Sarah a complete fit of the giggles by predicting that she would have a baby even though she was already old. When they caught her laughing, the Lord and his angels told her, "We'll give you something to laugh about!" And they called him *Isaac* (see Genesis 18:1-15; 21:1-6, AP).

An angel came twice to Manoah's wife to predict the birth of Samson. To be accurate, Samson's parents were unaware that their visitor was an angel until he left them via a flaming sacrifice sent up to the heavens (see Judges 13).

The angel Gabriel introduced himself clearly by name to Zechariah, while striking him speechless and sending him a son (see Luke 1:5-25). The same Gabriel continued in a gentler but no less shocking manner his annunciation to Mary that she had been chosen to give birth to the Son of God (see Luke 1:26-38).

———

In the case of Lot's visitation, the same angels who left Sarah laughing were sent next on an undercover mission to test the hospitality of the town of Sodom and find, if possible, ten righteous souls within it (see Genesis 18:16-33). Their visit tested Lot to the limits of his love, to the extent that he was willing to offer the bodies of his own offspring to save the skins of the men he had invited to dinner (see Genesis 19:1-11).

Lot was hospitable to a fault. Literally, to a fault. He was right and generous to invite the angels into his home, and of course he was correct to defend them from the violence that surrounded the house. Where Lot forgot himself was in limiting his generosity to the strangers and forgoing his duty of care to his daughters, treating them instead as mob fodder (see Genesis 19:8).

Ironically, the angels were more than able to defend themselves from the rioters outside the door (see Genesis 19:10-11). Lot's is the dilemma of the conscientious person: how to do right by everyone to whom love and duty is owed when their needs may compete.

If Lot passed the test with regard to the angels, he risked his daughters to do so. Yet he was still counted as righteous, which is not the same as perfect. Moreover, not every unexpected visitor is an angel in disguise.

———

My church's modest midweek Bible study is one of the most compelling ways we find ourselves entertaining strangers, sharing the gospel in profoundly personal and intimate detail. Some find us on purpose, through the calendar on the church's website or a friend's invitation. Others wander in looking for one of the anonymous meetings spread about the building, arriving at the wrong time or on the wrong day and finding us instead. Still others come looking for gas or money or other kinds of fuel. Most wait patiently through our prayers to make their true mission known. Those who arrive during our time of silent prayer, announcing themselves with a scraped door or a scuffed footstep, raise the hairs on our arms and make us wonder at the change of air and who has come to visit. When the building is open midweek for all sorts of anonymous meetings, there is vulnerability in the invitation to strangers looking for all kinds of salvation. But I am not sure how we would know whether those who come and go from time to time are, in fact, angels we have hosted unawares.

—————

Lately we have had to learn new habits of hospitality, such as staying six feet apart, withholding physical greetings, and wearing facemasks. We have had to learn how to identify friends and strangers by looking into their eyes. We have had to develop guidelines for how to approach someone who does not appreciate the safety measures we have in place because of the pandemic, or how to help someone understand that withholding physical affection does not diminish love.

Masks make some people uncomfortable, whether by wearing them or because they reduce the ability to recognize an angel, or anyone else, who visits our services. They put us in an embarrassing position when we fail to recognize someone whose eyebrows are raised above their cloth-covered nose, expecting our verbal embrace. They worry us when someone unknown shuffles in, and we cannot read their murmuring lips or lean in to understand them. Still, we accept that they are part of our compact with the Creator, not to do harm to those around us but to promote life and health and goodness in the name of Jesus.

—————

Someone has testified somewhere,
"What are human beings that you are mindful of
   them,
      or mortals, that you care for them?
You have made them for a little while lower than
   the angels;
      you have crowned them with glory and honor,
      subjecting all things under their feet."
                                            —HEBREWS 2:6-8

And must one be an angel to be worthy of welcome? What about the truly and utterly human stranger? (The psalmist, whom Hebrews quite nearly quotes above, elevates us even higher, calling us little lower than God [see Psalm 8:5].) What about the rest of us mortals, taking our hearts in our hands and our stomachs in our mouths as we grasp the handle of a new church, hoping for the best, huddled against lightning bolts, but not from God, and wondering how much of our secret identity shows beneath our Sunday clothes?

———

Everyone is welcome in the house of God, but not all behaviors are welcome. Everyone is welcome, and for the sake of safety and dignity, we set boundaries for how to be together respectfully. However, it is important to differentiate the actions and expressions that are really harmful from those that are idiosyncratic, unusual, or even uncomfortable to those unused to accommodating them but are ultimately the sign to an observant faith community of the compassion of an all-embracing Christ.

[Jesus said,] "Then the king will say to those at his right hand, 'Come, you that are blessed by my Father, inherit the kingdom prepared for you from the foundation of the world; for I was hungry and you gave me food, I was thirsty and you gave me something to drink, I was a stranger and you welcomed me.'"

—MATTHEW 25:34-35

We all have fallen short of the glory of the "All Are Welcome" sign. "Visitor profiling" of one sort or another is sometimes recommended as a congregational security measure. Looking for people who seem "out of place" or anxious, eager or desperate, over-zealous or unforthcoming feels like a blunt tool, though, when Jesus attracts Pharisees and centurions, foreigners and the faithful poor, women, children, tax collectors, and even the demon-possessed to hear his word and to touch the hem of his garment. Judging newcomers by their perceived ethnicity or liturgical background, their clothing, their gender expression, or their facial tics does not fit with the vision of the prophets, in which the dispossessed, eunuchs, foreigners, and outcasts will be joyful within the house of the Lord (see Isaiah 56:4-8).

———

When many young women were gathered in the citadel of Susa in custody of Hegai, Esther also was taken into the king's palace and put in custody of Hegai, who had charge of the women. The girl pleased him and won his favor, and he quickly provided her with her cosmetic treatments and her

portion of food, and with seven chosen maids from
the king's palace, and advanced her and her maids
to the best place in the harem. Esther did not reveal
her people or kindred, for Mordecai had charged her
not to tell.

—ESTHER 2:8-10

Esther must have known what had happened with Vashti,
how she had fallen from favor. She must, in any case, have been
terribly afraid, a young girl brought into the harem of the king.

Hegai was a eunuch, a man who knew that life is dangerous
and unpredictable, as people can be too. He realized the need
for somebody to tell the unspoken directions, rules, shortcuts,
escape routes, to show a little extra kindness, so Hegai decided
to help Esther.

Out of his otherness, he recognized hers, for all that she tried
to hide it, and took her into his belonging.

Does it sometimes take the experience of being a stranger to
know how to love the strangers in our midst?

Practicing hospitality may mean just that: accepting that there
will be trial and error. Sensible caution, protecting especially the
most vulnerable among us, balances against welcoming the most
vulnerable and unexpected visitors who approach us, remembering in whose name we open our doors to them.

Sarah laughed at the angels at Mamre, and Zechariah so
offended Gabriel by greeting his happy, if surprising, announce-
ment with disbelief that Gabriel decided to mute him for a time.
And we have talked already about Lot. All of these were considered righteous, blameless, and blessed, and we may be no better
than they at recognizing and welcoming angels, while maintaining the mutual love and care of our own household (see Hebrews

13:1-2). We do not want, like Lot, to have to choose between our family and the stranger who may or may not be an angel anyway.

But sometimes the unwelcome visitor is not a stranger to us at all.

———

> Jesus rebuked the demon, and it came out of him, and the boy was cured instantly. Then the disciples came to Jesus privately and said, "Why could we not cast it out?"
>
> —MATTHEW 17: 18-19

Modern interpretations have diagnosed some of the demons cast out by Jesus and his disciples in the Gospel accounts as conditions such as epilepsy (see Matthew 17:14-21; Mark 9:14-29; Luke 9:37-43) or madness caused by psychiatric disease (see Mark 5:1-20; Luke 8:26-39; compare Matthew 8:28-34). We surely know better than to ascribe evil intent to physical processes that afflict a person, but even in the most demoniac biblical accounts, the worth and appeal of the person to Christ are not diminished by their illness or apparent possession. The goal in each story is to restore the person to health by removing their affliction. Like his first disciples, we fall short of Jesus' power to complete a cure, but we can pray (see Mark 9:28-29).

The story is told that Jesus and his disciples had crossed the Sea of Galilee in a storm, which Jesus had quelled and calmed (see Mark 4:35-41; Luke 8:22-25). When they landed, they were greeted by a man who carried a storm within himself. Luke introduces him as "a man of the city" (Luke 8:27); he was a local boy. There were those close by who must have grown up with him. Perhaps he even had family living, but for now he was an outcast, living among the bones of the dead as though he had already left the land of the living. He mourned his own lost life, howling and hurting himself (see Mark 5:5). As soon as Jesus saw him, he commanded the unclean spirit to leave him alone.

Jesus saw the man and his need and addressed it as soon as he looked at him, calming the storm within him as readily as the storm that had threatened Jesus' boat on the inland sea. But the townspeople were as afraid of the man's cure as they were of his trouble.

> Then people came out to see what had happened, and when they came to Jesus, they found the man from whom the demons had gone sitting at the feet of Jesus, clothed and in his right mind. And they were afraid.
>
> —LUKE 8:35

The people who had no room for the man of their city when he was unclothed and out of his right mind, who locked him away among the tombs of the dead (Jesus would know something about the dread of that), also had no room for Jesus. Those who had first rejected and ejected their own from among them looked the Messiah in the face and sent him away.

> Then all the people of the surrounding country of the Gerasenes asked Jesus to leave them; for they were seized with great fear.
>
> —LUKE 8:37

While they were in Thyatira, lodging with Lydia, Paul and his companions spent a few uncomfortable days being followed about by an enslaved girl possessed of a "spirit of divination" (see Acts 16:16-18). Even though the young woman proclaimed the truth about them—that they served the Most High God and described the way of salvation—her repetitive and loud behavior was so profoundly annoying to Paul that he delivered her from the spirit, much to the chagrin of her owners and exploiters (see Acts 16:18-19). These businessmen saw to it that Paul and Silas were punished and imprisoned, but the irrepressible gospel, raised up by those apostles in song, enlisted the very crust of earth so that it quaked and the prison was shaken open. Paul's mercy toward the understandably terrified jailer led to his reconciliation, conversion, and the baptism of his whole family, so that the profits of the young woman's work were beyond reckoning (see Acts 16:19-34).

Yet we do not hear what happened to her after the spirit that allowed her to name the salvation she saw in Paul and Silas had been driven out of her.

> When the unclean spirit has gone out of a person, it wanders through waterless regions looking for a resting place, but it finds none. Then it says, "I will return to my house from which I came." When it comes, it finds it empty, swept, and put in order. Then it goes and brings along seven other spirits more evil than itself, and they enter and live there; and the last state of that person is worse than the first. So will it be also with this evil generation.
>
> —MATTHEW 12:43-45

We did not stop long enough in the young woman's story to discover her name or ask about her safety. We left her to the mercy of her owners and stray and homeless spirits. She was too loud, too annoying, and too obnoxious to hold our sympathy. I wonder where she ended up.

If we require our visiting strangers (and returning prodigals) to be perfect angels, what happens to everyone else?

———

- What is the profile of an undercover visiting angel?
- Who is demonized by your community?
- Who was in greater need of protection: Lot's visitors or his daughters? The Gerasene man or his neighbors?
- What kind of hospitality are you able to offer and to whom? Who offers it? Whom does it put at risk?
- Are there failures of hospitality that you regret?

———

Let love be genuine; hate what is evil, hold fast to what is good; love one another with mutual affection; outdo one another in showing honor. Do not lag in zeal, be ardent in spirit, serve the Lord. Rejoice in hope, be patient in suffering, persevere in prayer. Contribute to the needs of the saints; extend hospitality to strangers.

—ROMANS 12:9-13

FIVE

Love Thy Neighbor

For the whole law is summed up in a single commandment, "You shall love your neighbor as yourself."

—GALATIANS 5:14

To one community, the police may represent rescue; to another, danger. This is a reality of our society. If a congregation chooses to partner with police or other agencies for security, what message does it send to its neighbors, and what might it cost the church's mission?

The community police officer presenting the church security seminar back in the preface to this book told us that we should invest in first aid training: "We will not (we cannot) stop to help the bleeding," he told us. The focus of those first responders would not be distracted from their primary mission of finding and arresting or disabling the perpetrator of violence.

Of course, ministers ride along as police chaplains and many police officers volunteer at their churches. When disaster strikes, we call upon them to respond selflessly. Even so, as institutions with different heads and missions, our vocations diverge significantly in particular situations. In defining his department's responsibility in the moment of response to a violent event, the officer also reminded us of ours.

We know the story from Luke 10:30-35: An unidentified man was traveling from Jerusalem to Jericho on a treacherous and precipitous road. On the way, he was set upon by bandits, robbed, beaten, and left to die.

A priest and a Levite each slid by unnoticed, unharmed, and unstoppable. Then came the Samaritan man, the estranged cousin, the one whom the priest and the Levite might ordinarily cross the street to avoid.

The Samaritan man saw the bandits' handiwork, and instead of fear or revulsion, anger or satisfaction (that it was not him on the ground), he found himself moved with pity. Forsaking all other demands upon his time, attention, and money, he rescued the victim and found him room at the inn.

I suppose he was lucky that the robbers did not return while he was distracted by his labor of love.

The Samaritan man did what the community police officer was advising us not to do while the bandits were still nearby. But it was exactly what he said we should learn to do while the police took care of tracking the bandits down.

———

A couple of summers ago, my church put out lawn chairs in an attempt to engage the neighborhood. The idea was that church members would spend time simply sitting on the front lawn, chatting with passersby, and that those passing by, or waiting for the bus, might enjoy having a place to sit.

On the very first morning after the chairs were set out, I was excited to see that there were already people using two of them. A faithful church woman, Elaine, was deep in prayer with an unfamiliar man. As I pulled into the parking lot, they broke hands and looked up, allowing me to approach. We chatted a while, two white women and a tall, Black stranger whose life story we now knew in summary. We prayed a little more, and he asked for bus fare. We parted with mutual blessings.

As Elaine and I turned back toward the building, we saw a police cruiser pointed at us. The officer had his window down and was watching intently. "Did he ask you for money?" he wanted to know.

"He mostly wanted prayer," my faithful member replied, somewhat pointedly. I explained to the officer that this was a church, and that sometimes people came here asking for all kinds of help, and that sometimes I found it in my capacity and call to give it.

The police officer, white like us, answered that it was his job to be suspicious.[1]

———

When it comes to the familiar story of the good Samaritan, we are often encouraged by Bible studies and sermons to imagine ourselves in the shoes of the priest, the Levite, the Samaritan man—perhaps even, if one gets creative, the innkeeper. Amy-Jill Levine invites the reader to identify with the victim.[2] I even once heard Traci Blackmon address the criminally dangerous conditions of the road between Jerusalem and Jericho and the equivalent zip codes and avenues in modern America.[3] In the preaching tradition, we often straddle the divide between the original story and our current context, recasting characters and scenes. If we were to re-imagine this parable into our communities today, we might wonder whether or not the priest, the Levite, or even the Samaritan man should have called the police.

- If the police showed up and found the Samarian man crouched over the victim of bandits on the road from Jerusalem to Jericho, what do you imagine might happen next?
- Who in your congregation feels safer with a police presence? Who feels less safe?

———

An Episcopal friend and colleague, Alex Barton, is the priest in charge of a parish in a small and arguably rundown town on the shores of Lake Erie. His church attracts a variety of people to worship and to a regular community meal. It would be difficult for anyone to decide, based on traditional profiling, who would be an unusual visitor to the building and its events. That diversity is as we always claim that it should be for a Christian community, with our "All Are Welcome" signs.

Alex reminded me that while both of our (majority-white) churches talk a lot about anti-racism programming and social justice ministries, in fact, anti-racism should be built into everything that we do as the body of Christ. Our very being should be in contrast to the exclusionary, suspicious, unequally powerful, punitive, discriminatory, and divisive methods that modern society has found to protect the comfortable in the name of law and order.

Jesus, Alex said, preached good news to the poor, the meek, the captive, and the aggrieved. He held the powerful accountable, and he did not attempt to bring the two poles together. It is most likely beyond our ability to reconcile the suspicious and the suspect by the mediation of our ministries.

———

In the book of Judges, after Jephthah's horrible victory and terrible sacrifice, he became embroiled in a violent dispute in his own nation between the peoples of Gilead and Ephraim. The Ephraimites taunted the men of Gilead, but it was the Gileadites who instituted a purity test to determine who belonged with them and who should be destroyed.

> Then the Gileadites took the fords of the Jordan against the Ephraimites. Whenever one of the fugitives of Ephraim said, "Let me go over," the men of Gilead would say to him, "Are you an Ephraimite?" When he said, "No," they said to him, "Then say Shibboleth," and he said, "Sibboleth," for he could not pronounce it right. Then they seized him and killed him at the fords of the Jordan. Forty-two thousand of the Ephraimites fell at that time.
>
> —JUDGES 12:5-6

A faith community may choose to place a greeter alongside any guard. If the security detail is suspicious of a particular person based on ethnic or other profiling, then the congregation has someone whose privilege it is to vouch for that visitor—"We know her. She's safe."

But what if the Samaritan man was still a stranger, and we were the wounded ones? And what if there was no one to recognize his kind intentions in breaching the protocols that keep us apart?

———

It may be that contracting out its security concerns frees a congregation to concentrate on its ministries of love, healing, and the restoration of human life and relationships. But even as our prayers and community conversations and partnerships and calls for accountability continue, a church will want to ask difficult and often awkward questions before entering into such an arrangement.

- Does inviting a police or private security presence into a ministry setting invite them into the mission of the church, or does it submit the church to their mission control?
- If we contract out our internal security, can we be sure that the partners we employ will love our neighbors—as Jesus commanded—when they act on our behalf?
- When they stand in our name, will their presence and their actions be recognizable *to all who pass by* as accountable to the commandments of Christ?
- Will the priest, the Levite, the Samaritan interloper, and the repentant robber find themselves welcome, or will they see the police at the door and pass by on the other side?

———

Wanting to justify himself, [a lawyer] asked Jesus, "And who is my neighbor?"

—Luke 10:29

SIX

And Who Is My Neighbor?

You shall not profit by the blood of your neighbor:
  I am the LORD.
You shall not hate in your heart anyone of your
  kin. . . . but you shall love your neighbor as
  yourself: I am the LORD.

—LEVITICUS 19:16-18

The risk of violence is not equally distributed among our neighborhoods nor across faith communities. If your congregation enjoys the privilege of relative safety, are there ways in which it can share its benefits and shore up its neighbor's faith?

While all our church communities are debating safety, some houses of worship have more to worry about than others. White supremacy, racism, xenophobia, Islamophobia, anti-Semitism, homophobia, domestic violence, and misogyny have each played a role in mass shootings in America.

73

The murders of twenty-six people in Sutherland Springs, Texas, First Baptist Church in 2016 may have been linked to a domestic dispute.[1] A Sikh temple in Oak Creek, Wisconsin, was attacked in 2012 by a white supremacist, and Mother Emmanuel AME Church in Charleston was devastated when a young man with white supremacist leanings and learning wrought havoc on their midweek Bible study and the souls gathered there to pray in 2015.[2] In communities where the targets of multiple hateful ideologies intersect, the risk of violence is even higher.

In the summer of 2017, I had the pleasure of attending a writing week at the Collegeville Institute in Minnesota. It was there that I met Beth Kissileff, who is a writer from Pittsburgh and the wife of a Rabbi. I do not remember how, but at some point in our sabbath walk along the lakeside to the Stella Maris Chapel, we got onto the topic of pulpit safety. Beth's husband and I shared a position both as symbols and shepherds of our congregations. If violence were ever to invade, I confessed to Beth, I had already thought through a few scenarios. I was sure that her husband had done the same.

Fifteen months later, I returned from a sabbatical journey through Jordan, Palestine, and Israel. I couldn't help thinking of Beth when I was in Jerusalem, remembering what she had told me about the ease and comfort of staying in a place where sabbath was anticipated and where it was not countercultural to keep kosher.

The Saturday morning after I returned, a man with hatred in his heart attacked my friend's synagogue while her husband was inside. The man killed eleven people. Three of them were their friends from their congregation, and eight were from other congregations that shared the building at the Tree of Life in Pittsburgh, Pennsylvania.

———

When I finally met up with Beth again a little over a year after the killings, she described her grief, her faith, and her defiance in the face of evil. She has written of her opposition to the application of the death penalty to the killer's case: Death should not have the final word in this matter.[3] She has studied scripture and strengthened her faith, shoring it up against the onslaught of death and grief. If someone would kill a person simply for being Jewish, Beth said, then the most direct denial of their agenda is to live the Jewish faith with renewed life and vigor and to inspire others to do the same.

Others have done the same by coming to services (now held elsewhere) on Friday and Saturday—instead of only once a sabbath—to remember the dead or by taking on their friends' readings and new leadership roles to honor them.

The weekend after the murders, the hashtag #ShowupforShabbat invited people of all faiths and goodwill to attend synagogue services to let their neighbors know that they were supported, protected, and loved. It felt brave.

Beth and I talked about the incident in Halle, Germany, where a white supremacist (again) tried to gain entry to a synagogue on Yom Kippur. Unable to get in, he shot people at random in the surrounding streets, killing two.[4]

It should not take an act of bravery to attend worship or simply to be in the vicinity of a house of God.

Beth and I talked about the responsibility for a congregation to enact security measures to protect its own people, but I also wondered who would have suffered on our behalf if that gunman had come to my church and found its doors barred. I also had to wonder, as a mainstream white Christian minister in a mainstream, majority-white Christian congregation, would he even have come to my door? If not, what is my responsibility, from my place of privilege and relative safety, to alleviate the burden of risk that afflicts my neighbors' worship?

> All who believed were together and had all things in common; they would sell their possessions and goods and distribute the proceeds to all, as any had need. Day by day, as they spent much time together in the temple, they broke bread at home and ate their food with glad and generous hearts, praising God and having the goodwill of all the people. And day by day the Lord added to their number those who were being saved.
>
> —Acts 2:44-47

Programs such as #ShowupforShabbat or sharing secure buildings with more vulnerable worshiping communities might be appropriate ways of loving our neighbors as ourselves. A congregation that is relatively secure financially and socially might, instead of applying for a grant to improve its physical security, put its resources into seeking grants that would apply to every congregation in its neighborhood, each according to its need, sharing its capacity for security improvements with those at higher risk of violence and injury.

Even more urgent and at the heart of our gospel work is rooting out from among us the hateful ideologies and actions that have stolen the lives of the friends of my friend and have undermined our common good, which is the glorious sight of the image of God in the stranger across the street. "Seek the welfare of the city where I have sent you," Jeremiah prophesied to the people living among strangers (Jer. 29:7). And when Joseph worked for the Pharaoh of Egypt, stocking up grain against the famine to come, it was not only for the welfare of the royal household or even only the Egyptians; it fed the whole region and led to the reconciliation of Jacob's family (see Genesis 41–50).

Is it possible to weave compassion into the fabric of a disaster response plan and to prepare to love our neighbors as though it were an emergency?

- Who among your neighbors is most at risk of disruption or even violence during their worship services?
- What is your relationship to them?
- How might you offer to help shoulder their burden?

You shall not profit by the blood of your neighbor . . . but you shall love your neighbor as yourself: I am the LORD.

—LEVITICUS 19:16, 18

SEVEN

Through the Storm

The shades below tremble,
   the waters and their inhabitants.
Sheol is naked before God,
   and Abaddon has no covering.
He stretches out Zaphon over the void,
   and hangs the earth upon nothing.
He binds up the waters in his thick clouds,
   and the cloud is not torn open by them,
He covers the face of the full moon,
   and spreads over it his cloud.
He has described a circle on the face of the waters,
   at the boundary between light and darkness.

—JOB 26:5-10

We have all read the news reports and seen the grief brought home to our living rooms. It is more than likely that there are already those among you who have encountered violent trauma or terror. How do we care for those whose worst fears have already been realized or come far too close for easy comfort?

On Monday, February 27, 2012, my children had just returned from a teenage church weekend with friends they had known since elementary school, including a pair of brothers I had taught at Sunday school, now grown taller than me and bold in their faith and their friendship. I was working half-time at the parish, so I was catching up with some housework when my eldest texted me: "There's been a shooting."

Between my high schoolers using their phones without permission in class and my watching local TV news, we traded what little information we could gather through the morning about what was happening at their friends' school. Every time the television turned its cameras on the stream of students being released from Chardon High School, I scanned the screen for our people, our friends, our loved ones, hoping to be able to tell my children that Drew and his brother were safe.

As usual, the children were way ahead of me, texting after a couple of hours, "They're safe. They're good."

Six months later, a few dozen teens and chaperones spent the week sleeping nights on the floors of the church where I worked, spending our days outdoors building ramps for wheelchairs and fixing things, as we conducted a service mission to the parish's hometown. Drew spent the evenings playing the piano. He was open about the ongoing effects of that February morning and how he was working to incorporate them into his faith. Music helped. I remembered seeing him on the news the day after the shooting. He and some friends had gone that frigid evening to gather in the town square to play guitars and sing. He told me later they were singing, "Where Is the Love?" by the Black-Eyed Peas. I looked them up and found the lyrics to be mourning and wondering, reverent and rebellious, defiant and loving.

Several years later, Drew Gittins and I met up at the café in the cathedral complex, just along the corridor from where I had taught him and his brother in Sunday school, and we talked about that high schoolers' church weekend and the morning after.

Now a law student, Drew recalled a jumble of reactions and emotions in the moments after the shooting in the school cafeteria. Following the lockdown protocol, students piled into a classroom and waited. They were getting most of their information from Twitter, so there were conflicting reports about what had actually happened. Later they learned that six of their fellow students had been shot by another student. Three of them died within a day, and another suffered life-altering injuries. A teacher ran the attacker off the property.

Drew described wondering at least once during the lockdown whether it would become necessary to die to protect his friends.

"No one has greater love than this, to lay down one's life for one's friends" (John 15:13).

Drew's faith had prepared him to ask himself whether he would, whether he could, even if he did not have the answer.[1]

But when we talked about how the church might protect a child's faith as well as their physical presence in the sanctuary or at Sunday school, Drew did not want to get too hung up on the threat of an evil event intruding. There are enough risks in the world. Instead, he described how the church could be instrumental in providing a framework and foundation for finding meaning and grace come what may. After the trauma of his high school coming under attack from one of their own and the challenge of how to respond in the moment and beyond, Drew found a call to become more Christlike, to double down on service, the love that defeats evil.

The church can help or hinder that call, he said. The church needs to invest its children with the knowledge of the love of God, the peace that passes understanding, and the grace that will attend them in all situations, even those situations we pray will never come.

———

Who will separate us from the love of Christ? Will hardship, or distress, or persecution, or famine, or nakedness, or peril, or sword? As it is written,

"For your sake we are being killed all day long;
we are accounted as sheep to be slaughtered."

No, in all these things we are more than conquerors through him who loved us. For I am convinced that neither death, nor life, nor angels, nor rulers, nor things present, nor things to come, nor powers, nor height, nor depth, nor anything else in all creation, will be able to separate us from the love of God in Christ Jesus our Lord.

—ROMANS 8:35-39

My eyes will flow without ceasing,
    without respite,
until the LORD from heaven
    looks down and sees.
My eyes cause me grief
    at the fate of all the young women in my
    city. . . .
I called on your name, O LORD,
    from the depths of the pit;

you heard my plea, "Do not close your ear
   to my cry for help, but give me relief!"
You came near when I called on you;
   you said, "Do not fear!"
—LAMENTATIONS 3:49-51, 55-57

Michele Gay and Alissa Parker are the cofounders of Safe and Sound Schools. Their organization's mission is "to support school crisis prevention, response, and recovery, and to protect every school and every student, every day."[2] They created and sustain this work because their lives have accommodated unthinkable tragedy since Alissa's eldest daughter, Emilie, and Michele's youngest, Josephine, were murdered at their elementary school in Sandy Hook, Connecticut, in 2012.

Then was fulfilled what had been spoken through
the prophet Jeremiah:
"A voice was heard in Ramah,
   wailing and loud lamentation,
Rachel weeping for her children;
   she refused to be consoled, because
      they are no more."
—MATTHEW 2:17-18

While their nonprofit is functionally secular, Michele and Alissa talked with me about the role that faith continues to play in their response and recovery from that personal crisis and tragedy.

Both Michele and Alissa grew up in families and communities where faith was vital. Michele's parents were active members of the Catholic church, and they also exposed her to a deliberately and progressively interfaith community in Columbia, Maryland. Alissa is a member of The Church of Jesus Christ of Latter-day Saints, a famously large and close-knit faith community.

In the book she wrote about her eldest daughter's continuing presence in her life, *An Unseen Angel*, Alissa tells the story of calling Michele, using the RSVP number on Emilie's invitation to Josephine's birthday party. As soon as she introduced herself, she writes, "Michele said, 'I hope you believe in heaven, because they are up there together.' "[3]

The two women were bound together not only by tragedy but by also the shared hope that Michele articulated in that first phone call—more than hope, a conviction that their daughters were living with God, and that their grieving parents and family members would one day be reunited to them. Their mutual faith was one of the balms that they were able to offer each other and the foundation of what became a fast friendship, a sisterhood.

Speaking within church settings about the role of faith is one thing; negotiating it as part of a public presentation on behalf of a secular body is another. But Michele pointed to the "privilege" of telling one's own story—no one can fault a mother for describing the faith that has helped her to survive the indescribable. And others have not been shy about sharing their own faith— praying openly, sending cards and prayers and poems, showering the families of the children lost at Sandy Hook with the love of God. In a twist of our small world, Drew Gittins was among a group of students who drove from Chardon, Ohio, to Newtown, Connecticut, just a couple of weeks after the tragedy, meeting at a church with local middle- and high-school peers to share their own experiences of grief and healing, bringing blankets and love.[4]

Alissa described the ripples of devastation that spread from the epicenter of violence and loss. The deluge of prayer and care that rushed back in was astonishing and a little bewildering. It was a reminder that the love of God is more overwhelming and enduring than evil, and God's love shows itself in all sorts of unexpected ways, through all sorts of unexpected people.

Faith is certainly not a panacea for all that afflicts us. But even in our deepest grief and anger so many of us find ourselves reaching back toward God, for compassion if not for comfort, looking for the love that death cannot drown (see Song of Solomon 8:7). Faith—querulous, questioning, even quaking—can be a lifeline in the most stretching of times.

Better: Christ provides a lifeline, walking like a ghost through the storm to tender the conviction of things not seen, the hope of heaven.

> When evening came, the boat was out on the sea, and he was alone on the land. When he saw that they were straining at the oars against an adverse wind, he came towards them early in the morning, walking on the sea. He intended to pass by them. But when they saw him walking on the sea, they thought it was a ghost and cried out; for they all saw him and were terrified. But immediately he spoke to them and said, "Take heart, it is I; do not be afraid." Then he got into the boat with them and the wind ceased.
>
> —MARK 6:47-51

Alissa and Michele agreed when we talked together that they can see the difference that faith has made to their recovery since the tragedy at Sandy Hook Elementary. What they did not say, but what I might, is that they are signs themselves, these mothers of daughters and children of God, pointing to the painful and beautiful promise of resurrection. They also reminded me how important it is to have trauma-informed care and compassion in faith-based communities. Not everyone wants to tell the story of how their faith was tested to its limits or show their scars to strangers or neighbors or even pastors. It is up to the leadership to provide clear and compassionate content warnings when difficult subjects might come up, or when safety drills might be upsetting, or when youth might need help avoiding an activity without giving out their life story to their peers.

"Do not hold on to me," Jesus said to Mary when she first found him in the garden after his resurrection. "I have not yet ascended to the Father" (John 20:17). He needed a moment.

Serene Jones, writing on *Trauma and Grace*, has observed that "to be human is to live only a hairbreadth from the unbearable."[5] The incarnation of a Christ whose violent and helpless death is countered by resurrection but whose resurrected body remembers its wounds is the strongest demonstration of God's comprehension and compassion for the traumatized person.[6]

Learning the patterns of trauma, Jones suggests, equips us to "touch traumatized imaginations" with this grace.[7] Ritual, remembrance, and the recasting of the trauma of Christ's crucifixion in the shadow of resurrection have potential to contribute to healing even as they recognize the persistence of old injuries and assaults and the need for continuing gentleness and care.[8]

- What storms still frighten your spirit?
- How has your faith helped you weather difficult, even tragic, events and seasons?
- How might your church learn about and practice trauma-informed faith formation?

Now who will harm you if you are eager to do what is good? But even if you do suffer for doing what is right, you are blessed. Do not fear what they fear, and do not be intimidated, but in your hearts sanctify Christ as Lord. Always be ready to make your defense to anyone who demands from you an accounting for the hope that is in you; yet do it with gentleness and reverence.

—1 PETER 3:13-16

EIGHT

And a Child Shall Lead Them

[Jesus] took [the children] up in his arms, laid his hands on them, and blessed them.

—MARK 10:16

Deciding how to protect our children without burdening them, freeing them from fear to faith, takes honest reckoning and courageous conversation among those charged with their nurture and inspiration.

When my child was very young, I was tucking her into bed one night, and she was distressed. I asked why, and the reply was that at any moment, an asteroid might smash into the earth and destroy it, ending all life and all knowledge of life in an instant. Rational arguments about probabilities, space stations, forecasts, warnings, and probabilities again did nothing to soothe the young soul. "But you can't tell me it *can't* happen," she insisted. And, the implication was, if the extremely unlikely did, in fact, befall, then nothing I could say or do would protect my beloved child from the consequences.

The Revelation to John is a vision that defies easy explanations. It describes the anxieties and real trauma of his people and his era, but it also transcends history in its existential anger, pain, and hope for the eventual end of oppression and death under the reign of Christ, the Lamb of God.

> A great portent appeared in heaven: a woman clothed with the sun, with the moon under her feet, and on her head a crown of twelve stars. She was pregnant and was crying out in birth pangs, in the agony of giving birth. Then another portent appeared in heaven: a great red dragon, with seven heads and ten horns, and seven diadems on his heads. His tail swept down a third of the stars of heaven and threw them to the earth. Then the dragon stood before the woman who was about to bear a child, so that he might devour her child as soon as it was born. And she gave birth to a son, a male child, who is to rule all the nations with a rod of iron. But her child was snatched away and taken to God and to his throne; and the woman fled into the wilderness, where she has a place prepared by God, so that there she can be nourished for one thousand two hundred sixty days.
>
> —REVELATION 12:1-6

A woman is giving birth, and a dragon waits to snatch the child away to its doom. The scene is pregnant with symbolism: Matriarchs and patriarchs, apostles and martyrs, Christ and the church, the whole people of God labor to bring forth something hopeful, something good, something lively, while danger crouches at their side, waiting for their most vulnerable moment, ravenous for their security, hungry to remove their hope.

The entire scene shows how fear becomes a monster, how anxiety dogs us, how our imaginations allow real and valid concerns, threats, and perils to take on the features of a child's nightmare.

At the crucial moment a hero enters, Michael the Archangel. The child is whisked away to heaven, the woman is comforted, the armies of angels defeat the dragon's horde. God's mercy will not be denied, yet I wonder who nurses the child in the absence of his mother. I wonder who heals the heaviness of her breasts and tends to the emptiness of her arms. There is victory here, but it does not solve all of the problems raised by the initial threat of the dragon at the door.

Children already know that the world is dangerous. They do not need their fears magnified; their imaginations will take care of that without encouragement. They see dragons in their sleep.

The Revelation is realistic about the dangers of the world, but it is adamant that God's better angels will have the victory.

———

"God will provide," Abraham told Isaac as they labored up the mountain, Isaac beneath a bundle of firewood and Abraham under the terrible burden of believing that he was about to sacrifice his child (see Genesis 22:1-14). The whole scene resonates with notes of trust and fear comingled. How could Abraham simultaneously trust God and believe that God might demand the life of his son?[1] What did the boy make of his father's firm but evasive answer to his question about where the sacrificial lamb was to come from?

Abraham tied him to the pyre Isaac had carried up the hill himself and raised the knife. The trust that Isaac had in his father, with his assurances that "God will provide," must at that moment have been hanging by a hair.

————

All I could do to comfort my child the night she learned about intergalactic asteroids was to remind her that love endures no matter what. Even if the world ends, she is beloved. Even if we die, we are alive in Christ.

It was not really enough for her or for me; it is what we parents live with, trusting that God understands how angry it sometimes makes us that our children know that death is as certain as love in this world.

————

The challenge of inspiring our children with confidence, sustaining their fearless faith and life, and countering the messages of anxiety and panic that the world generates, while committing to their physical and spiritual safety, is one that adults have to find a way to take on without burdening children with their own protection.

We might explore the story of young David, who, upon hearing of the giant Goliath, emboldened himself with memories of the many times God had protected him and led him to defeat dangerous wild animals. The seasoned fighters around him tried to teach him their tips for staying safe, loading him up with armor and weaponry beyond his maturity to wield. David trusted instead in the history of his faith and his experience of God's providential care to save him.

David told Saul,

> "The LORD, who saved me from the paw of the lion and from the paw of the bear, will save me from the hand of this Philistine."
>
> —1 SAMUEL 17:37

David said to Goliath,

> "You come to me with sword and spear and javelin; but I come to you in the name of the LORD of hosts, the God of the armies of Israel, whom you have defied. This very day the LORD will deliver you into my hand, and I will strike you down and cut off your head; and I will give the dead bodies of the Philistine army this very day to the birds of the air and to the wild animals of the earth, so that all the earth may know that there is a God in Israel, and that all this assembly may know that the LORD does not save by sword and spear; for the battle is the LORD's, and he will give you into our hand."
>
> —1 SAMUEL 17:45-47

It is a story we have told our children for generations, encouraging them to look beyond the foolish arms races of their elders to trust instead in their innate and providential relationship with God. It has become at once prophetic and problematic in an era when children are taught that they must protect themselves by slinging books and shoes at monsters that might invade their safety.

The tensions between trust and fear, nonviolence and active resistance to evil, praying for our enemies and slaying giants, believing in the providence of God and knowing that sometimes the worst befalls us anyway are nowhere more starkly highlighted than in our relationship with our children, the questions they ask, and the stories that we tell them.

How to keep our children safe in body, soul, and spirit is perhaps the most fraught question we can ask God, scripture, and ourselves. "No one has greater love than this, to lay down one's life for one's friends" (John 15:13) we teach them, and we hope to God they will never have to consider its call upon their lives.

We want to teach our children the truth of the Christ who boldly told his disciples, "Do not fear those who kill the body but cannot kill the soul" (Matt. 10:28). We want them to grow strong enough to take up the cross and follow Jesus for themselves, Jesus who said, "If any want to become my followers, let them deny themselves and take up their cross and follow me" (Mark 8:34).

But first they need the chance to grow up.

———

- What does your church teach its children in word and in deed about God's loving care and provision for them and their families?
- What are the burdens of the world that your children and young people bring with them to church?
- Does the church accidentally add to or intentionally lighten those burdens?

———

A month after the horrific murders at Marjory Stoneman Douglas High School in Parkland, Florida, young people and their parents, grandparents, godparents, and supporters staged the March For Our Lives in cities across the country and the world. It appeared for a moment as though the country might stop listening only to gun advocates and start listening to the disturbing, dynamic, and brave voices of young people who had survived the worst that could happen at high school (way worse than many of us imagined when we were at school).

The courage and resilience of so many young people were an inspiration. Something seemed to be shifting in the atmosphere. The rallies of March 2018 featured the voices of teenagers, loud and unedited, followed by six long minutes of silent grief, remembering how long it took a mass shooter to claim seventeen lives.[2] The adults in the crowd hung their heads, shuffled their feet, and marched behind the young people, wondering why it had not occurred to them to lead.

Of course, there was also the wry and mostly silent acknowledgment that other children in other cities had been begging for our attention for years without notice. They were on our collective conscience too.

About halfway through our march in Cleveland, I found myself on East Ninth Street directly behind a woman with a young child in a backpack carrier like the one I had used when my children were younger. Too small to walk so far, the little one's legs and feet hung from the carrier, bouncing and dancing with her mother's stride. A sign attached to the outer fabric of the child's traveling nest said, "My preschool class does lockdown drills."

I wanted to fall to my knees on the spot and repent of my dismal stewardship of her world, but the crowd swept me on. And as it did, I wondered, *What if her sign had read, "My Sunday school class does lockdown drills"?*

"And a little child shall lead them" (Isa. 11:6).

Specialists in child psychology and school safety are beginning to question the proliferation and intensification of the lockdown drills and active shooter trainings that have swept this country's schools in the last ten years or so. Some sources suggest that there may be little benefit—and unknown harm—in traumatizing children now just in case the world decides to do it later.[3]

A friend's church was tested in full view of their children when a woman who had a mental illness tailgated a family buzzed through a security door as they were dropping off their children for choir on a Wednesday night. The woman attacked a student babysitter with a knife while the children's instructor cried out for help and the screams of the little ones grew louder. The Director of Spiritual Education crossed the room and subdued the attacker, placing her own body between danger and the children in her care. My friend, the newly arrived interim pastor, heard the change in the tenor of shrill background noise and knew that something was terribly wrong.

A young woman was left with a long road to recovery. Another woman was once again arrested and remanded for the consequences of her violent illness. A number of families and children were shaken and traumatized because their elaborate security precautions—precautions that some had thought quite over-the-top to begin with—failed to keep them safe. A pastor will live with the memory of gathering the children like chicks under the wings of a mother hen, scurrying them away to safety, and attempting to spread calm until their own mothers or others came to collect them.

The following Sunday, the Rev. Jessica MacMillan addressed her congregation. She named the violation of their safe and sacred space, and she named the healing power of prayer. She relived some of her own reactions and responses: hearing the tenor of the children's high-pitched voices change and taking a moment to register what it meant, feeling haunted by storms and the shadow of death and remembering that these too are part of life, the bodily memory of trauma.

She named the ongoing responsibility of the church to its children: "We love our children, and when they come into this house of worship, they are all of our children and they will be protected. When they are afraid, they will be comforted. When they are traumatized, we will help them heal."

She named some of the things that grounded her, even in the moments following the attack, as she and a few other adults huddled into a play tent with the children as they waited for the crime scene to be cleared:

> The way one young child can reach out to another
> even when they are both terrified.
> How a small warm hand feels like connection to life.
> A child's scared eyes that melt into hope when a
> parent arrives to comfort them.
> The sound of *Dona Nobis Pacem* reverberating off
> the canvas of a tent when everyone is scared.
> Hearing *Runaway Bunny* read by a girl who has just
> experienced trauma.
> Praying for someone who has just caused harm,
> because the children asked me to.[4]

When we spoke some months later, Jessica lifted up once more that moment when the child asked her to lead a prayer for the woman they had just witnessed wreaking havoc among them. This is what they had been taught, and now, with the innocence of a profound and simple faith, they were returning the lesson to their teachers.

Whatever measures are enacted to protect Sunday school classrooms and youth spaces from harm must not make the children carry the wood for their own sacrifice or burden them with armor so heavy that they can no longer lift their heads to see the hope that Jesus offers. A church can help build up those resources that will stand them in good stead whatever shadowy valleys they may walk through: teaching them to hold one another's hands, to pray, even for their enemies, as Jesus taught us.

- How are your children and young people being encouraged and enabled to clothe themselves in a faith that fits and will carry them through stormy times, whether at church or in the world?
- How does the church equip its children both to resist evil and to pray for their enemies?
- What do you learn about faith, fear, courage, and forgiveness from the prayers of the children and young people in your life and in your church?

The wolf shall live with the lamb,
    the leopard shall lie down with the kid,
the calf and the lion and the fatling together,
    and a little child shall lead them.
                                    —ISAIAH 11:6

NINE

Many Sparrows

For my thoughts are not your thoughts,
  nor are your ways my ways, says the LORD.
For as the heavens are higher than the earth,
  so are my ways higher than your ways
  and my thoughts than your thoughts.
For as the rain and the snow come down from
    heaven,
  and do not return there until they have watered
    the earth,
making it bring forth and sprout,
  giving seed to the sower and bread to the eater,
so shall my word be that goes out from my mouth;
  it shall not return to me empty,
but it shall accomplish that which I purpose,
  and succeed in the thing for which I sent it.
                              —ISAIAH 55:8-11

It is time to reflect on what we have learned about ourselves, our gospel priorities, and our immediate challenges. This closing chapter also offers the opportunity to imagine how we can change the world around us so that we can write a new story for the future.

We live upon a landscape shaped by violence. Abel's blood cries out from the soil (see Genesis 4:10). Rizpah cannot bear to leave the bones of her children (see 2 Samuel 21:1-14). Rachel remains unconsoled (see Jeremiah 31:15; Matthew 2:18). The cross, now empty, reminds us of the depths of our capacity for inhumanity and God's paradoxical and merciful bent toward humanity. The gun violence that surrounds us is a spiritual issue; it's a question of life and death. It is a cultural conundrum, a political and ideological battleground, and a public health problem.

The public health model of gun violence prevention and reduction often points to improvements in vehicular safety over the years. The introduction of speed limits, evaluation of driver education, and cultural changes in attitudes about alcohol consumption and driving evolved in parallel with technical improvements to the vehicles themselves: seat belts, airbags, and crumple zones. Still, beside country roads and interstate highways, far too often you will see flowers and crosses, teddy bears and flags representing thoughts and prayers.

"Thoughts and prayers" has become a symbol for the least we can do, an empty gesture of sympathy without action. But a church runs on prayer. How can our thoughts and prayers be used to change the landscape around us to make it less dangerous, less deadly? How can we turn this around?

Abel's blood prayed to God from beneath the ground. Rizpah's ritual was a political as well as a spiritual protest. Each was a far cry from Jesus' admonition to the hypocrites and their show-prayers, meant for human applause rather than divine engagement and requiring no follow-up from the prayer (see Matthew 6:5; Mark 12:40).

Nehemiah's people prayed for the protection of their work restoring Jerusalem; they also set a guard (see Nehemiah 4:9). Jonah prayed when there was nothing else left for him to do, buried in the belly of a fish. When his prayer was answered, God expected him to act upon it (see Jonah 2:1; 3:3). The prayers of the righteous, James insisted, are powerful and should not be neglected (see James 5:13-18).

During the time of King David, the Gibeonites sought violent reparation for the evil that they said was done against them by Saul, and David allowed them to slaughter seven of Saul's sons and grandsons. Rizpah, concubine to Saul and mother to two of the dead, watched over their bodies, which were exposed upon the hillside, mourning their loss and the way in which they had been given up by the king. She used her grief as a protest and her funerary observances as a silent critique of the powers that had used her sons as pawns in their own bloody feuds (see 2 Samuel 21:1-14).

Of course it is the place and the call of the church to remember and pray for the dead and the endangered, for the bereaved and the injured, for the innocent and for the guilty. It is a core part of our mission to offer thoughts and prayers. But our prayers must include confession and the promise of repentance, hope and the plea for strength to do what is right, a calling to account of those in power—especially when we hold power ourselves—and the admonition of evil and yearning for the kingdom of God.

Our prayers hold space for grief, lament, anger, and regret. If they are to hold out hope, they should also show us where we can move a little closer to the will of God for the world.

———

When Pilate saw that he could do nothing, but rather that a riot was beginning, he took some water and washed his hands before the crowd, saying, "I am innocent of this man's blood; see to it yourselves."

—MATTHEW 27:24

What good is it, my brothers and sisters, if you say you have faith but do not have works? Can faith save you? If a brother or sister is naked and lacks daily food, and one of you says to them, "Go in peace; keep warm and eat your fill," and yet you do not supply their bodily needs, what is the good of that? So faith by itself, if it has no works, is dead.

—JAMES 2:14-17

In Lent, 2019, the Beating Guns tour came to Cleveland. Shane Claiborne and Michael Martin brought a traveling smithy to Pilgrim Congregational United Church of Christ on the west side of the city and set up the furnace outside. Inside the church, David Eggert, co-founder of God Before Guns,[1] the local sponsor of the event, described how he had legally purchased an AR-15 rifle from a stranger he had found through online ads, making the exchange in an empty parking lot. The gun was sawed up and fed into the fire, and participants lined up to hammer it out on the anvil until it was transformed into a garden tool: a death-dealing instrument beaten into a life-growing implement after the vision of the prophets (see Micah 4:3; Isaiah 2:4).[2]

Later that summer, gun prevention organizations borrowed space in church parking lots, including mine, to collect signatures on a petition to tighten the background-check laws in Ohio that had allowed David to buy an AR-15 from a stranger in a private sale.

Thoughts and prayers can lead to action. Art can breed inspiration. Symbols offer hope—especially when they become a vehicle for God's grace, changing the world for the better.

———

[Jesus] called the crowd with his disciples, and said to them, "If any want to become my followers, let them deny themselves and take up their cross and follow me. For those who want to save their life will lose it, and those who lose their life for my sake, and for the sake of the gospel, will save it. For what will it profit them to gain the whole world and forfeit their life? Indeed, what can they give in return for their life? Those who are ashamed of me and of my words in this adulterous and sinful generation, of them the Son of Man will also be ashamed when he comes in the glory of his Father with the holy angels."

—MARK 8:34-38

Some churches advertise that they have armed security. If a church chooses to disarm for the sake of the gospel, should it advertise that fact?

There are those who believe that "gun-free zones" are soft targets for mass shooters, but some research from Johns Hopkins University calls that into question. To my mind, the tragic phenomenon of school shootings would appear at least anecdotally to support the report's finding that the majority of mass shooting targets are chosen because of the perpetrator's prior relationship with the location or with the victims rather than because of a calculation of resistance or risk.[3]

The choice to go gun-free might be based in economic or legal reasons; if a church cannot afford the cost of armed security, it might not feel like a choice at all, in which case there may be little that they wish to say about it. But if the choice to go gun-free is based in the gospel, if it is part of the church's commitment to the Way of the Cross, then it may well become part of the messaging of a church that follows the Prince of Peace. If a congregation affirms the promise of the psalm, "Yea, though I walk through the valley of the shadow of death, I will fear no evil" (Ps. 23:4, KJV), adding, *and I shall not contribute to its shade or to its bones*, then it may want to broadcast that hope, faith, and steadfastness to its neighbors.

If a church delights in removing violence from within its borders and the currency of death from its economy, why not preach that gospel? "Let your gentleness be known to everyone. The Lord is near" (Phil. 4:5). Are we afraid to display our vulnerability? That is another question. "See, I am sending you out like sheep into the midst of wolves; so be wise as serpents and innocent as doves" (Matt. 10:16).

———

> When he opened the fifth seal, I saw under the altar the souls of those who had been slaughtered for the word of God and for the testimony they had given; they cried out with a loud voice, "Sovereign Lord, holy and true, how long will it be before you judge and avenge our blood on the inhabitants of the earth?"
>
> —REVELATION 6:9-10

After a particularly deadly week of mass gun violence in August 2019, my congregation began sending out condolence cards first to our cousin churches and then to other faith communities in places where tragedy had taken place. We sent our sympathy and our prayers, and we pledged to work toward ending gun violence and the factors that contribute to it. Each time we signed a card, we were confronted with our own commitment and call to work toward the world we proclaim in the gospel, which falls under the reign of the Prince of Peace.

I was surprised by how many churches and faith communities replied to us, sending cards or leaving voice mails at the church. These strangers' grateful acceptance of our love and our work in turn cemented the covenant we had signed to do more than write down our thoughts and prayers.

———

At the beginning of this book, I quoted the following from the Catechism of the Episcopal Church:

> Q. How does the Church pursue its mission?
> A. The Church pursues its mission as it prays and worships, proclaims the Gospel, and promotes justice, peace, and love.[4]

Prayer and worship are the primary means by which we move ourselves and the world toward unity with God and one another in Christ. Hosting meaningful vigils; praying regularly for issues of gun violence and other threats to the good of God's people; using art, music, sacred space, sacred speech, and all the tools of liturgy that the church has at its disposal are inherent in our work toward a more peaceful, grace-filled world as we proclaim the gospel and promote justice, peace, and love. Making policy decisions and modeling the life we seek, free from the fear of gun violence, is another tool for dismantling the systems of sin and destruction that threaten our peace of mind, body, and spirit. The opportunities to make a difference in the world around us are as multivalent as the gifts and members of the body of Christ.

- One church might include in its weekly or monthly prayer list the names of persons who have been affected by gun violence.
- Churches have plenty of opportunity to promote gun safety at home by making information available to parents, grandparents, and guardians about safe gun storage and the high risks of leaving weapons open to children's experimentation, accident, or impulsive use. Sunday schools could use their registration forms to invite families to check their gun ownership and storage status.[5]
- Churches can address in preaching and teaching the high proportion of gun deaths that occur by suicide—around 60 percent—and choose to investigate and invest in ways of supporting those in mental and emotional distress.[6]
- Some churches may have the resources to undertake or underwrite a gun buy-back program.
- One church may decide to try "investor activism" or "shareholder advocacy" to move the needle on gun sales. The Episcopal Church at its 2018 General Convention passed a resolution to that effect, arguing that

> dioceses, church organizations, and individual Episcopalians investing in the publicly traded stock of gun manufacturers and retailers could act to effect change in these companies through

the practices of shareholder advocacy to do everything in their power to minimize lethal and criminal uses of their products.[7]

- Another church might decide that investing in gun manufacture sends a mixed message and choose to add such companies to their ethical investment screen instead.[8]
- A church might address some of the underlying social causes of gun violence, including poverty, racism, mental illness, and despair.
- The church may choose to live into its ancient call to be a place of "sanctuary"—whatever that might mean in its current context—a backdrop of peace when tensions are high.
- I have heard of ministries that visit the scenes of violent crimes to pray for healing to come to those street corners and homes, to turn them from places of fear to places of the fierce faith that resists evil.

In 2016, at the prompting of my friend, the Reverend C. Eric Funston, I began making orange clergy stoles to participate in Wear Orange Weekend, a national witness against gun violence. In 2018, when I attended an event organized by the Episcopal Church's Bishops United Against Gun Violence, a sea of orange stoles of various designs clashed brightly against the bishops' scarlet chimeres and purple shirts as the parents of a student killed at Marjory Stoneman Douglas High School in Parkland, Florida, reminded us that we do not pray for the impossible when we come together in this way; "for God all things are possible" (Matt. 19:26).[9]

Of course, Jesus began by saying, "For mortals it is impossible." That is why we pray, to join ourselves to God's power, instead of relying on our own. And if God is with us, who can stand against us? (See Romans 8:31.)

———

As we come to the end of our time together, consider the following:

• What are the problems, risks, or threats that you are seeking to address as a congregation?
• How pressing are they?
• What does the gospel say about them?
• What are your non-negotiable gospel values?
• Do the proposed solutions conform to those values?
• Whom shall we fear?

———

[Jesus said,] "Do not fear those who kill the body but cannot kill the soul; rather fear him who can destroy both soul and body in hell. Are not two sparrows sold for a penny? Yet not one of them will fall to the ground apart from your Father. And even the hairs of your head are all counted. So do not be afraid; you are of more value than many sparrows."

—MATTHEW 10:28-31

ACKNOWLEDGMENTS

I owe more thanks than I will ever remember to offer. Where I have fallen short, please forgive me.

My parish of the Church of the Epiphany, Euclid, Ohio, is a source of constant inspiration and gospel accountability and love. My thanks to you all, especially our Deacon, Josh Butler, and to Elaine, now of ever-blessed memory, for allowing me to share our lawn-chair story.

My diocesan and interfaith colleagues likewise lift my spirits and keep me curious.

A number of people have assisted with this project through their support, introductions, and conversations: Alex Barton, Margaret D'Anieri, Charles Eduardos, Michele Gay, Drew Gittins, my Bishop, Mark Hollingsworth, Jr., Beth Kissileff, Tracey Lind, Jessica MacMillan, Michelle Moore, Shari Nacson, Alissa Parker, Donald Rawls, John Shelley, and Nancy Wittig to name but some. Kristine and David Eggert and their God Before Guns board and organization are a wonderful source of courage and encouragement, and I am indebted to C. Eric Funston for the orange stole idea.

Writing is not a solitary activity, and I am blessed by the company I keep. I could not find the words without my writing partner, Christina G. Kukuk, and they would not find their way in the world without my editors, Joanna Bradley Kennedy and Michael S. Stephens, and the wonderful team at Upper Room Books. Of course any errors or omissions remain my own.

For my godchildren, I pray peace in your time.

To my husband, Gareth, thank you for loving and helping me every day.

To my children, thank you. I love you. You continue to teach me everything I know about the world and its profound potential for good.

To God be the glory.

APPENDIX

A Biblical Litany for Churches Pursuing Peace

Leader: A new heart I will give you, and a new spirit I will put within you;

People: I will remove from your body the heart of stone and give you a heart of flesh.

Leader: Happy is the one who is never without fear, but one who is hard-hearted will fall into calamity.

People: A new heart I will give you, and a new spirit I will put within you.

Leader: Merciful God, conform our will to yours; transform our hearts.

People: I will remove from your body the heart of stone and give you a heart of flesh.

Leader: Take us not out of this world, but remove the worldliness from our thoughts and our desires.

People: A new heart I will give you, and a new spirit I will put within you.

Leader: God give us a heart to love you perfectly, and to heed
            your perfect will.

**People: I will remove from your body the heart of stone and
            give you a heart of flesh.**

Leader: Defend us from our enemies, O God; let us find our
            refuge in you.

**People: A new heart I will give you, and a new spirit I will
            put within you.**

Leader: Give us authority to trample scorpions and pick up
            snakes, but let us prefer your love to our power.

**People: I will remove from your body the heart of stone and
            give you a heart of flesh.**

Leader: Teach us to forge plowshares instead of pistols, prun-
            ing hooks instead of long guns; save us from living and
            dying by the sword.

**People: A new heart I will give you, and a new spirit I will
            put within you.**

Leader: We will give over our idols of metal to the moles and
            the bats, to the rust and the moth, and set our heart on
            your Word.

**People: A new heart I will give you, and a new spirit I will
            put within you.**

Leader: Save us from the time of trial; keep us as your eye stays
            on the sparrow.

**People: I will remove from your body the heart of stone and
            give you a heart of flesh.**

Leader: Give us such perfect love for our neighbor as casts out
            prejudice, fear, or contempt.

**People: A new heart I will give you, and a new spirit I will
            put within you.**

Leader: Mold us as peacemakers, for we are your children.

People: **I will remove from your body the heart of stone and give you a heart of flesh.**

Leader: Suffer the little children to come to you; lift them up and bless them, as you love them, Lord Jesus.

People: **A new heart I will give you, and a new spirit I will put within you.**

Leader: Forgive those whom we struggle to forgive or to forget.

People: **I will remove from your body the heart of stone and give you a heart of flesh.**

Leader: Forgive us our trespasses.

People: **A new heart I will give you, and a new spirit I will put within you.**

Leader: A broken and contrite heart, O God, you will not despise.

People: **I will remove from your body the heart of stone and give you a heart of flesh.**

Leader: The Lord is my light and my salvation; whom shall I fear?

People: **Wait for the Lord; be strong, and let your heart take courage.**

Leader: Now to him who by the power at work within us is able to accomplish abundantly far more than all we can ask or imagine, to him be glory in the church and in Christ Jesus to all generations, forever and ever.

People: **Amen.**

The litany quotes or refers to the following scripture passages: Deuteronomy 6:5; Psalm 51:17; 27:1; 27:14; 143:9; Proverbs 28:14; Isaiah 2:4; 2:20; Ezekiel 26:36; Micah 4:3; Matthew 5:9; 5:48; 6:13; 6:19, 21; 10:29-31; 26:52; Mark 10:13-16; 16:18; Luke 10:19; 11:4; 23:34; John 17:15; Romans 12:12; Ephesians 2:20-21; 1 John 4:18.

APPENDIX

Leader's Guide

Thank you for choosing to read and discuss *Whom Shall I Fear? Urgent Questions for Christians in an Age of Violence*. While each chapter contains its own set of discussion questions and passages to ponder, you may find this leader's guide and its extended questions and prompts helpful in planning conversations with congregational leadership or other small groups.

Because these topics are weighty, I recommend taking a full ten sessions to review the book. However, some chapters naturally hang together, and at the end of this guide you will find suggestions for organizing your discussions into fewer sessions. Every congregation's situation is unique, from its people to its position in the community. I encourage you to adapt as you have need: You know best what your congregation wants and needs from this book.

Read the entire book before you begin. Make notes of where the themes and questions of the book intersect with the particular concerns and hopes of your congregation. Pay attention to your own feelings so that you can become a non-anxious presence for your people during your time together.

Designate someone to be the chaplain for each session. It can be the same person each time or a rotation of qualified people. Chaplains should read the entire book in advance, so that they know if there are particular sessions that require them to take care of themselves first.

For each session, it is most useful for participants to have read the sections under discussion. Make sure everyone has access to a copy of the book, and encourage them to make notes as they read so they can bring their questions, prayers, and other responses to the conversation. Set aside some minutes at the end of each meeting for people's reflections from their reading that have not been addressed elsewhere in your conversation.

This leader's guide cannot anticipate your community's unique need for trauma-informed care during your conversations. If you are uncertain about any aspect of that, you may wish to consult with community partners with expertise in the field to create a comfortable and kindly environment for these sessions.

It is also important to keep in mind that these sessions are not designed or equipped to lead a congregation to make firm decisions about its security. There are many other agencies and expert advisors that can help with that.

Instead, this book encourages Christians to remember first the love of God, shared with the whole world. Let your prayerful engagement with the Word of God expressed in scripture and the body of Christ guide your conversation and give you confidence to talk together about your values, your prayers, your ministry, and your mission to God's church and God's world.

Although we haven't met, you are in my prayers as you lead your faith community through this time together, toward God, toward peace.

—Rosalind C. Hughes

Session 1. Preface and Introduction

Preparation

Re-read the preface and introduction. Consider the questions at the end of the preface and the introduction. Choose some questions for the focus of your discussion.

Introduction

Provide a welcome and make introductions as needed. Introduce the chaplain to the group and explain that if anyone needs personal conversation or prayer during or after the session, the chaplain is available to them. Encourage people to take care of their own health and well-being: They can take a break at any time without excuse or explanation if they feel overwhelmed by the topic.

Remind the group that they are not gathered today to make practical decisions or solve particular dilemmas about security issues in the church but primarily to pray and reflect upon God's Word to your church.

Opening Prayer

Ask the group to share—aloud or silently—their prayer concerns and requests. Take a moment of silence, and then read the first and last verses of Psalm 27:

> The LORD is my light and my salvation;
>   whom shall I fear?
> The LORD is the stronghold of my life;
>   of whom shall I be afraid?
> I believe that I shall see the goodness of the LORD

in the land of the living.
Wait for the LORD;
    be strong, and let your heart take courage;
    wait for the LORD!

Discussion

The preface describes the author's experience of tension between good, sound, secular advice on safety in her church and the dynamics of her congregation and its understanding of the gospel.

- Ask members of the group if they have any similar experiences or insights.
- Look at the questions at the end of the section. How would you define your church's core mission and ethos?

The introduction begins the discussion how we approach the dilemma of being in the world but not of the world (see John 15:19; 17:14-16). Before we apply our prayer and understanding to questions of violence, it encourages us to recognize that God understands our dilemmas and affirms our honest and faithful attempts to live into the gospel we proclaim.

- Choose one of the examples presented to craft a conversation about the compromises we make with that gospel and how they affect your congregation's reading of the Word of God.
- Use the questions at the end of the introduction to discuss where you know yourselves to be already divided between the world and the kingdom of heaven and how God's radical understanding, forgiveness, and strength might help you to reconcile your beliefs, prayers, and actions.

Closing Prayer

Invite those present to share their prayers silently or aloud, and then draw them together in the Lord's Prayer, the prayer in which Jesus taught us to pray, "thy kingdom come."

Remind participants to keep one another in prayer and to read the next chapter before you meet again.

Session 2. Chapter One: Behold, I Stand at the Door and Knock

Preparation

Re-read chapter one and pay particular attention to the meditation exercise on pages 26 and 31–32. Choose either the Nehemiah story (pp. 27–29) or the *Light of the World* story (pp. 29–31) for further discussion. If the question of locked or unlocked doors is an active one in your congregation, you may wish to appoint a small group to write up your spiritual and theological findings from this discussion to present to the body tasked with making decisions about your doors.

Introduction

Continue to reassure participants that they may prioritize their own health and safety by taking a break without excuse or explanation if necessary. Introduce the chaplain for the session.

Opening Prayer

Ask the group to share—aloud or silently—their prayer concerns and requests. Take a moment of silence, and then read the first and last verses of Psalm 27:

> The LORD is my light and my salvation;
>   whom shall I fear?
> The LORD is the stronghold of my life;
>   of whom shall I be afraid?
> I believe that I shall see the goodness of the LORD
>   in the land of the living.
> Wait for the LORD;
>   be strong, and let your heart take courage;
>   wait for the LORD!

Discussion

This chapter begins the imaginative work of immersing ourselves in the world of the Bible and translating it to our present circumstances. Remind the group that this is not a book of practical advice on how, whether, and when to lock and unlock doors. Rather, it explores what our approach to those practicalities teaches the world about the gospel.

- What images from the biblical stories and verses stand out or resonate?

Take a few minutes to engage in the meditation exercise about locked doors as a group (pp. 26 and 31–32).

- Encourage people to share their insights: Where was Jesus for them?

Choose either the Nehemiah story (pp. 27–29) or the *Light of the World* image (pp. 29–31) for further discussion.

- What message do your doors proclaim to those within and without them?

Closing Prayer

Invite those present to share their prayers silently or aloud, and then draw them together in the Lord's Prayer, the prayer in which Jesus taught us to pray, "thy kingdom come."

Remind participants to keep one another in prayer and to read the next chapter before you meet again.

Session 3. Chapter Two: Do Not Be Overcome by Evil

Preparation

Re-read chapter two. Choose a few of the questions from the end of the chapter for your group's discussion.

Introduction

Remind participants that they may prioritize their own health and safety by taking a break if necessary. Introduce the chaplain for the session.

Opening Prayer

Ask the group to share—aloud or silently—their prayer concerns and requests. Take a moment of silence, and then read the first and last verses of Psalm 27:

The LORD is my light and my salvation;

whom shall I fear?
The LORD is the stronghold of my life;
of whom shall I be afraid?
I believe that I shall see the goodness of the LORD
in the land of the living.
Wait for the LORD;
be strong, and let your heart take courage;
wait for the LORD!

Discussion

Introduce the question that is the crux of this chapter:

- Are there are limits to Jesus' instruction to "turn the other cheek"?

In the story of Moses presented in the chapter, violence appears to lead only to further violence, even when it is intended as an interruption to violence.

- When we are faced with the threat of violence or evil, does the commandment to nonviolent resistance change?
- Discuss the questions you chose from the end of the chapter.
- Finally, What does it mean to "not be overcome by evil, but overcome evil with good" (Rom. 12:21)?

Closing Prayer

Invite those present to share their prayers silently or aloud, and then draw them together in the Lord's Prayer, the prayer in which Jesus taught us to pray, "lead us not into temptation."

Remind participants to keep one another in prayer and to read the next chapter before you meet again. The next chapter deals more specifically with guns and violence.

Session 4. Chapter Three: Who Will Heal Malchus's Ear?

Preparation

Re-read chapter three. Choose one or more of the Gospel accounts of the scene in the garden of Gethsemane for discussion (Matthew 26:30-56; Mark 14:26-50; Luke 22:39-53; John 18:1-11). If the question of guns in church is an active one in your context, consider appointing a small group to report on your spiritual and theological gleanings and further questions from this conversation to present to the body tasked with making decisions.

Introduction

Remind your people that they are gathered to pray and reflect upon God's Word together, rather than to make specific security decisions. As established, participants may prioritize their own health and safety by taking a break if necessary. Introduce the chaplain for the session.

Opening Prayer

Ask the group to share—aloud or silently—their prayer concerns and requests. Take a moment of silence, and then read the first and last verses of Psalm 27:

> The LORD is my light and my salvation;
> whom shall I fear?

The L<small>ORD</small> is the stronghold of my life;
   of whom shall I be afraid?
I believe that I shall see the goodness of the L<small>ORD</small>
   in the land of the living.
Wait for the L<small>ORD</small>;
   be strong, and let your heart take courage;
   wait for the L<small>ORD</small>!

Discussion

Guns, gun ownership, and gun violence can be hot-button top-ics. Depending upon your context, beginning with the questions about participants' relationships with guns (see p. 44), while encouraging mutual listening and respect, may be necessary to set the scene for a productive and loving discussion.

After giving that conversation some set time, read the scene or scenes in the garden of Gethsemane you have chosen (Matthew 26:30-56; Mark 14:26-50; Luke 22:39-53; John 18:1-11).

- What Jesus was trying to teach his disciples and his ene-mies in that moment?
- Does the concept of "prophetic action" help you to recon-cile the "two swords" passage in Luke 22:35-38 with the events of Jesus' arrest?
- What is the relationship of the worship of the church with the events of the garden, that scene between the Last Sup-per and the Cross and Resurrection? And how does that inform your answer to the question, *Do deadly weapons belong in the house of God, the home of the body of Christ?*

Closing Prayer

Invite those present to share their prayers silently or aloud, and then draw them together in the Lord's Prayer, the prayer in which Jesus taught us to pray, "deliver us from evil."

Remind participants to keep one another in prayer and to read the next chapter before you meet again.

Session 5. Chapter Four: Hospitality Is Not Only for Angels

Preparation

Re-read chapter four. If appropriate, invite leaders of your hospitality/greeters'/ushers' ministries to share their stories during this session.

Introduction

As usual, reassure participants that they may prioritize their own health and safety by taking a break if necessary. Introduce the chaplain for the session

Opening Prayer

Ask the group to share—aloud or silently—their prayer concerns and requests. Take a moment of silence, and then read the first and last verses of Psalm 27:

> The LORD is my light and my salvation;
>   whom shall I fear?
> The LORD is the stronghold of my life;
>   of whom shall I be afraid?

I believe that I shall see the goodness of the LORD
   in the land of the living.
Wait for the LORD;
   be strong, and let your heart take courage;
   wait for the LORD!

Discussion

As it says at the beginning of the chapter, "The balance between hospitality to our own congregation and to the visiting stranger can be delicate. How can a church be genuinely and lovingly welcoming, offering sanctuary to those who need it the most?"

Lot's story, the experience of the Gerasenes and their outcast, Paul's exorcism of the annoying but truthful spirit all have their echoes in our own experience of hospitality and its shortcomings.

- What stories of hospitality does your congregation celebrate?
- What failures of hospitality would you prefer to forget, and what can you learn from them instead?
- What is your gospel policy for welcoming the stranger, for "I was a stranger and you welcomed me" (Matt. 25:35)?
- If there are limits to your hospitality, for the safety of others, what is your responsibility to follow up or "refer on" and find a welcome for the rejected visitor elsewhere?

Closing Prayer

Invite those present to share their prayers silently or aloud, and then draw them together in the Lord's Prayer, the prayer in which Jesus taught us to pray, "give us this day our daily bread."

Remind participants to keep one another in prayer and to read the next chapter before you meet again.

Session 6. Chapter Five: Love Thy Neighbor

Preparation

Re-read chapter five. If your congregation or small group participated in justice rallies following recent high-profile incidents of police brutality, that may inform your imaginative engagement with this chapter. If your congregation or this discussion group includes law enforcement professionals, they may be able to weigh in on the questions of authority and mission that conclude the chapter.

Introduction

As usual, remind participants that they may prioritize their own health and safety by taking a break if necessary. Introduce the chaplain for the session.

Opening Prayer

Ask the group to share—aloud or silently—their prayer concerns and requests. Take a moment of silence, and then read the first and last verses of Psalm 27:

> The LORD is my light and my salvation;
>   whom shall I fear?
> The LORD is the stronghold of my life;
>   of whom shall I be afraid?
> I believe that I shall see the goodness of the LORD
>   in the land of the living.

Wait for the LORD;
be strong, and let your heart take courage;
wait for the LORD!

Discussion

This chapter asks some admittedly awkward questions about the church's relationship to the state authorities that surround it and often support it.

- What is your community's relationship with local authorities?
- Is your congregation of one heart and mind in this response, or are there differences among you? On what are these differences based?
- Who in your congregation feels safer with the police or private security around, and who feels less safe?
- Can you build bridges between different communities and areas of authority while maintaining the independence of the church and the accountability of everyone concerned?

Closing Prayer

Invite those present to share their prayers silently or aloud, and then draw them together in the Lord's Prayer, the prayer in which Jesus taught us to pray, "forgive us our trespasses, as we forgive those who trespass against us."

Remind participants to keep one another in prayer and to read the next chapter before you meet again. Be advised that the next chapter includes reflections from a survivor of religious violence.

Session 7. Chapter Six: And Who Is My Neighbor?

Preparation

Re-read chapter six. The risk of violence is not equally distributed among our neighborhoods, nor across faith communities. The perception of danger is not always consistent either. Before this session, you may wish to research crime statistics in the neighborhood of your church and surrounding areas.

Introduction

Remind participants that they may prioritize their own health and safety by taking a break if necessary. This session will include reflections from a survivor of religious violence. Introduce the chaplain for the session.

Opening Prayer

Ask the group to share—aloud or silently—their prayer concerns and requests. Take a moment of silence, and then read the first and last verses of Psalm 27:

> The LORD is my light and my salvation;
>   whom shall I fear?
> The LORD is the stronghold of my life;
>   of whom shall I be afraid?
> I believe that I shall see the goodness of the LORD
>   in the land of the living.
> Wait for the LORD;
>   be strong, and let your heart take courage;
>   wait for the LORD!

Discussion

While this session, like the others, is not intended to produce practical decisions about the congregation's security, it may spark ideas that members of the group would like to follow in the wake of these conversations.

- Is your church located in a "safe" neighborhood or one associated with more risk of violence?
- Is the church considered a "safe space" within your neighborhood?
- What real and urgent risks does your congregation face, and are they similar, elevated, or less than those of the people who surround you?
- What does it mean to your congregation to "seek the welfare of the city where I have sent you" (Jer. 29:7)?
- How can you partner with other faith communities and community organizations to lessen the risks of violence to all of those within your circle of concern?
- How will you partner with others to reduce the impact of racism, anti-Semitism, gender-based violence, Islamophobia, or other currents that are of particular concern in your area?

Closing Prayer

Invite those present to share their prayers silently or aloud, and then draw them together in the Lord's Prayer, the prayer in which Jesus taught us to pray, "thy kingdom come, thy will be done on earth as it is in heaven."

Remind participants to keep one another in prayer and to read the next chapter before you meet again. Be advised that the next chapter includes interviews with survivors of school violence, including bereaved parents.

Session 8. Chapter Seven: Through the Storm

Preparation

Re-read chapter seven.

Introduction

Continue to reassure participants that they may prioritize their own health and safety by taking a break if necessary. Any invitation to reflect on trauma must contain permission to refrain from telling stories that the person is unready or unwilling to share. This session includes a review of interviews with survivors of school violence, including bereaved parents. Introduce the chaplain for the session.

Opening Prayer

Ask the group to share—aloud or silently—their prayer concerns and requests. Take a moment of silence, and then read the first and last verses of Psalm 27:

> The LORD is my light and my salvation;
> whom shall I fear?
> The LORD is the stronghold of my life;
> of whom shall I be afraid?
> I believe that I shall see the goodness of the LORD
> in the land of the living.
> Wait for the LORD;
> be strong, and let your heart take courage;
> wait for the LORD!

Discussion

In this chapter, Drew, Michele, and Alissa reflect on the role of faith in helping a person to survive and recover from trauma.

- What resonates, and what challenges you in their stories?
- If a participant identifies times when the church has failed to acknowledge their trauma, what can you as a congregation learn from those times?

Michele and Alissa set up www.safeandsoundschools.org as a positive way to work toward their own healing by interrupting violence before it can hurt others.

- How can the work of the church—reaching out its hands in love—help to heal the hearts of those doing the work as well as those receiving its benefits?

Closing Prayer

Invite those present to share their prayers silently or aloud, and then draw them together in the Lord's Prayer, the prayer in which Jesus taught us to pray, "thy kingdom come, thy will be done on earth as it is in heaven."

Remind participants to keep one another in prayer and to read the next chapter before you meet again. Be advised that the next chapter includes a scene of church violence witnessed by children.

Session 9. Chapter Eight: And a Child Shall Lead Them

Preparation

Re-read chapter eight. You may wish to invite members of your children and youth ministries to this discussion. And if there are parents, grandparents, other caregivers, or young people involved in your group discussions, be prepared to listen for their burdens of fear and anxiety.

Introduction

Reassure participants that they may prioritize their own health and safety by taking a break if necessary, remembering that this chapter includes the description of a violent and traumatic incident witnessed by children. This session is not designed to address particular security questions about children's and youth ministries but to reflect upon the faith that we introduce to our children through our words and actions as we care for them. Introduce the chaplain for the session.

Opening Prayer

Ask the group to share—aloud or silently—their prayer concerns and requests. Take a moment of silence, and then read the first and last verses of Psalm 27:

> The LORD is my light and my salvation;
>   whom shall I fear?
> The LORD is the stronghold of my life;
>   of whom shall I be afraid?
> I believe that I shall see the goodness of the LORD

> in the land of the living.
> Wait for the LORD;
>> be strong, and let your heart take courage;
>> wait for the LORD!

Discussion

- What do the stories of Isaac and David teach us about the burdens that our children carry through the world of today, and how can we relieve them?
- What are the lessons you glean from the Rev. MacMillan's well-protected church's encounter with violence, and the ministry of its children to one another and to their adults afterwards?
- How do you hope to equip your children and youth to live faithfully and fearlessly in an uncertain and troublesome world?

Closing Prayer

Invite those present to share their prayers silently or aloud, and then draw them together in the Lord's Prayer, the prayer in which Jesus taught us to pray, "deliver us from evil."

Remind participants to keep one another in prayer and to read the next chapter before you meet again.

Session 10. Chapter Nine: Many Sparrows

Preparation

Re-read chapter nine and the Biblical Litany for Churches Pursuing Peace. Prepare copies of the litany, write it on a whiteboard or

flip chart, or set it up for screen sharing. Set aside time at the end
of the session to pray the litany together.

Introduction

In this final session, do not flag in making sure that participants are
reassured that they may prioritize their own health and safety by
taking a break if necessary. Introduce the chaplain for the session.

Opening Prayer

Ask the group to share—aloud or silently—their prayer concerns
and requests. Take a moment of silence, and then read the first
and last verses of Psalm 27:

> The LORD is my light and my salvation;
>   whom shall I fear?
> The LORD is the stronghold of my life;
>   of whom shall I be afraid?
> I believe that I shall see the goodness of the LORD
>   in the land of the living.
> Wait for the LORD;
>   be strong, and let your heart take courage;
>   wait for the LORD!

Discussion

While this session, like the others, is not intended to produce
practical decisions about the congregation's security, it may spark
ideas that members of the group would like to follow in the wake
of these conversations.

The final chapter of the book moves from considering our
reactions and responses to the violence around us to wondering

how we can reduce it, changing the landscape around us as when the prophets promise to, " 'Prepare the way of the Lord, make his paths straight. Every valley shall be filled, and every mountain and hill shall be made low, and the crooked shall be made straight, and the rough ways made smooth, and all flesh shall see the salvation of God' " (Luke 3:4-6, after Isaiah 40:3-5).

- What might the thoughts and prayers of your discussion group lead to in terms of action, engagement, and the inspiration of your broader community to address and reduce violence?
- Use the ideas in the chapter as a jumping-off point for your own work, and do not neglect to invite God's blessing on your efforts.

End with your renewed commitment to pray for one another.

Closing Prayer

Use the litany at the end of the book as the centerpiece of a closing liturgy, by itself or with the Lord's Prayer, in which Jesus reminds us to pray that "the kingdom, the power, and the glory are yours, now and forever." Amen.

Suggested Arrangements for Fewer Sessions:

1. Sessions 1 and 2 (The preface, introduction, and chapter one) may be combined as an introduction to the themes and practice of the book.
2. Sessions 3 and 4 (chapters two and three) may be combined as an introduction to the tradition of Christian nonviolence, followed by its application to the more pointed question of guns in churches. This session would

include some weighty discussion, and a break for prayer and respite in the middle is recommended.

3. Sessions 5, 6, and 7 (chapters four through six) focus on our relationship with strangers and outside groups, from random church visitors to state authorities and other faith communities that surround us. One way of organizing an extended session would be to focus first on our approach to the stranger among us, through the lenses of chapters 4 and 5, then after a break for prayer and respite to return and wonder about the experiences of our neighbors and how they are similar or different to our own.

4. Sessions 8 and 9 (chapters seven and eight) are grounded in the experiences of children, young people, and those who love them. These chapters may call up strong emotions, but, taken together, they form a framework for facing honestly the burdens that our children carry in the age of school lockdown drills and how the church can work to relieve them, acknowledging the trauma that the continual specter of violence causes to many of our congregants.

5. Session 10 (chapter nine) concludes your time together by imagining a future in which we do the prophets' work of "preparing the way of the Lord," removing violence and obstacles to peace from before us. Plan a closing worship service to draw your prayers together and celebrate your commitment to peace.

NOTES

Preface

1. For more on fear as a marketing tool, see Scott Bader-Saye, *Following Jesus in a Culture of Fear*, The Christian Practice of Everyday Life (Grand Rapids, MI: Brazos Press, 2007), esp. ch. 1.

2. Aaron Karp, *Estimating Global Civilian-Held Firearms Numbers*, June 2018 Briefing Paper, Australian Government Department of Foreign Affairs and Trade (Geneva: Small Arms Survey, 2018), http://www.smallarmssurvey.org /fileadmin/docs/T-Briefing-Papers/SAS-BP-Civilian-Firearms-Numbers .pdf, accessed February 2, 2021.

3. The author's search for the first use of this familiar phrase has not determined its origin.

4. *The Book of Common Prayer and Administration of the Sacraments and Other Rites and Ceremonies of the Church, Together with the Psalter or Psalms of David, According to the use of The Episcopal Church* (New York: The Seabury Press, 1979), 854–55.

Introduction: Whom Shall I Fear?

1. Scott Bader-Saye, *Following Jesus in a Culture of Fear*, The Christian Practice of Everyday Life (Grand Rapids, MI: Brazos Press, 2007), 59.

2. C. S. Lewis writing as N. W. Clerk, *A Grief Observed* (Greenwich, CT: The Seabury Press, 1963), 7.

3. See Bader-Saye, *Following Jesus in a Culture of Fear*, ch. 3, esp. 42–44.

Chapter Two: Do Not Be Overcome by Evil

1. See, for example, Michelle Kailey, "Redeeming the Atonement: Girard-ian Theory," *Denison Journal of Religion* 8, art. 7 (2008). Available at: http://digitalcommons.denison.edu/religion/vol8/iss1/7, accessed August 14, 2020.

2. See also Athena E. Gorospe, *Narrative and Identity: An Ethical Reading of Exodus 4* (Leiden: Brill, 2007), 160–61.

3. Henry Chadwick gives Ignatius's date of death as "before A.D. 117" in *The Early Church*, rev. ed. (London: Penguin Books, 1993), 30.

4. Ignatius of Antioch, *Epistle of Ignatius to the Romans*, ch. 4 in *Ante-Nicene Fathers, Volume I: The Apostolic Fathers with Justin Martyr and Irenaeus*, ed. Alexander Roberts and James Donaldson (1885, repr. Boston: Hendrickson, 1995), 75.

5. Justin Martyr, *The First Apology of Justin*, ch. 16 in *Ante-Nicene Fathers, Volume I*, 168; Irenaeus, *Against Heresies*, bk. 4, ch. 34, sect. 4 in *Ante-Nicene Fathers, Volume I*, 512. See also David Kopel, "Christian Pacifism Before Constantine," SSRN Electronic Journal (2008): 10.2139/ssrn.1144924. Available at: https://www.researchgate.net/publication/228277490 _Christian_Pacifism_Before_Constantine, accessed July 22, 2020.

6. Irenaeus, *Against Heresies*, bk. 4, ch. 34, sect. 4 in *Ante-Nicene Fathers, Volume I*, 512.

7. See Scott Bader-Saye, *Following Jesus in a Culture of Fear*, The Christian Practice of Everyday Life (Grand Rapids, MI: Brazos Press, 2007), 129.

8. Eberhard Bethge explains the circumstances of the essay's creation in his foreword to Dietrich Bonhoeffer, *Letters and Papers from Prison* (London: SCM Press, 1953), 11.

9. Bonhoeffer, *Letters and Papers from Prison*, 135–37.

10. Bonhoeffer, *Letters and Papers from Prison*, 137.

11. Bonhoeffer, *Letters and Papers from Prison*, 136–37.

12. Walter Wink, *The Powers That Be: Theology for a New Millennium* (New York: Doubleday, 1998), 42.

13. This quandary is explored by William R. Jones in *Is God a White Racist? A Preamble to Black Theology* (Boston, MA: Beacon Press, 1973, rev. 1998), esp. pt. 1.

14. Kelly Brown Douglas, *Stand Your Ground: Black Bodies and the Justice of God* (Maryknoll, NY: Orbis Books, 2015), 187–88.

15. Bonhoeffer, *Letters and Papers from Prison*, 135–38, esp. 138.

16. Walter Wink expands upon this in a section titled, "On Not Becoming What We Hate," in *The Powers That Be*, 122ff.

Chapter Three: Who Will Heal Malchus's Ear?

1. Saint Ambrose of Milan, "Exposition of the Holy Gospel According to Saint Luke," bk. X, sects. 53, 66–70 in *Exposition of the Holy Gospel According to Saint Luke, with Fragments on the Prophecy of Esaias*, trans. Theodosia Tomkinson, 2nd ed. (Etna, CA: Center for Traditionalist Orthodox Studies, 2003), 409, 413–15.

2. Cyril of Alexandria, *Commentary on Luke*, Sermon 145 (Pickering, OH: Beloved Publishing, 2014), 433–36.

3. Cyril of Alexandria, *Commentary on Luke*, Sermon 148, 442–45, esp. 444-45.

4. Notes on Luke 22:35-38 in *The New Oxford Annotated Bible*, ed. Michael D. Coogan, 3rd ed. (New York: Oxford University Press, 2001), 140NT.

Chapter Five: Love Thy Neighbor

1. I told this story in my sermon for Ash Wednesday, 2020, at the Church of the Epiphany, Euclid, OH: http://rosalindhughes.com/2020/02/26/ash-wednesday-grace-is-not-in-vain.

2. Amy-Jill Levine, *Short Stories by Jesus: The Enigmatic Parables of a Controversial Rabbi* (San Francisco: HarperOne, 2014), 90.

3. Traci Blackmon, "And What About the Road," Festival of Homiletics, Minneapolis, MN, May 16, 2019.

Chapter Six: And Who Is My Neighbor?

1. Sarah Mervosh, "Mass Shootings at Houses of Worship: Pittsburgh Attack Was Among the Deadliest," *New York Times*, October 27, 2018, https://www.nytimes.com/2018/10/27/us/mass-shootings-church-synagogue-temple.html, accessed August 11, 2020.

2. Associated Press, "A List of Some US House of Worship Shootings since 2012," October 27, 2018, https://apnews.com/0b2a73fdcf944d19aaafa 620bb1d94c0, accessed August 11, 2020.

3. Beth Kissileff, "The Jewish Answer to How to Punish the Pittsburgh Synagogue Shooter," Religion News Services, February 27, 2019, https://religionnews.com/2019/02/27/the-jewish-answer-to-how-to -punish-the-pittsburgh-synagogue-shooter/, accessed August 11, 2020.

4. BBC News, "German Synagogue Shooting Was Far-Right Terror, Justice Minister Says," October 10, 2019, https://www.bbc.com/news/world -europe-50003759, accessed August 11, 2020.

Chapter Seven: Through the Storm

1. Drew Gittins has written his own account of this day. See Drew Gittins, "Survivors Still Suffer: I Survived a School Shooting," *The Chimes* (Capital University student newspaper, Bexley, OH), March 15, 2018, https://cuchimes.com/03/2018/survivors-still-suffer-i-survived-a-school -shooting/, accessed March 1, 2021.

2. "Our Mission," *Safe and Sound Schools,* https://www.safeandsound schools.org/about-us/our-mission/, accessed March 1, 2021.

3. Alissa Parker, *An Unseen Angel: A Mother's Story of Faith, Hope, and Healing after Sandy Hook* (Salt Lake City, UT: Ensign Peak, 2017), 45.

4. Cliff Pinckard, "Chardon High School Students, Teachers, Parents Use Blankets to Comfort Newton, Conn., Students," *Cleveland.com,* https:// www.cleveland.com/metro/2013/01/chardon_high_school_students_t .html, accessed August 24, 2020.

5. Serene Jones, *Trauma and Grace: Theology in a Ruptured World,* 2nd ed. (Louisville: Westminster John Knox, 2019), 18.

6. Jones, *Trauma and Grace,* 22.

7. Jones, *Trauma and Grace,* xxii.

8. Jones, *Trauma and Grace,* 73.

Chapter Eight: And a Child Shall Lead Them

1. Nahum M. Sarna explores this scene thoroughly in *Understanding Genesis: The World of the Bible in the Light of History* (New York: Schocken Books, 1995), including the observation that: "The narrative as it now

stands is almost impatiently insistent upon removing any possibility of misunderstanding that God had really intended Abraham to sacrifice his son," 161.

2. Dakin Andone, "Emma Gonzalez Stood on Stage for 6 Minutes—The Length of the Parkland Gunman's Shooting Spree," *CNN*, March 25, 2018, https://www.cnn.com/2018/03/24/us/march-for-our-lives-emma -gonzalez/index.html, accessed February 4, 2021.

3. See, for example, https://everytownresearch.org/school-safety-drills/ on the need for a trauma-informed approach to children's safety and security measures. Accessed July 24, 2020.

4. Jessica MacMillan, "Service and Sermon Notes for November 24, 2019," shared with the author by email.

Chapter Nine: Many Sparrows

1. See https://www.godbeforeguns.org.

2. Claiborne and Martin describe their ministry in Shane Claiborne and Michael Martin, *Beating Guns: Hope for People Who are Weary of Violence* (Grand Rapids, MI: Brazos Press, 2019). I wrote about the Cleveland event for RevGalBlogPals. See Rosalind C. Hughes, "The Pastoral is Political: Beating Guns," April 29, 2019, https://revgalblogpals.org /2019/04/29/the-pastoral-is-political-beatingguns/.

3. Daniel W. Webster, Cassandra K. Crifasi, Jon S. Vernick, Alexander McCourt, "Concealed Carry of Firearms: Fact vs. Fiction," Center for Gun Policy and Research, Bloomberg American Health Initiative, Johns Hopkins, https://www.jhsph.edu/research/centers-and-institutes /johns-hopkins-center-for-gun-policy-and-research/_archive-2019/ _pdfs/concealed-carry-of-firearms.pdf. See p. 8.

4. *The Book of Common Prayer and Administration of the Sacraments and Other Rites and Ceremonies of the Church, Together with the Psalter or Psalms of David, According to the use of The Episcopal Church* (New York: The Seabury Press, 1979), 855.

5. See Tyler Kingkade, "How Moms Are Quietly Passing Gun Safety Policy through School Boards," *NBC News*, February 10, 2020, https:// www.nbcnews.com/news/us-news/how-moms-are-quietly-passing-gun -safety-policy-through-school-n1132891, accessed February 12, 2021.

6. UC Davis Health reports that in 2018, 61 percent of deaths from fire-
    arms in the US were by suicide, and that "firearms are the means in
    approximately half of suicides nationwide." "What You Can Do: Facts
    and Figures," *UCDavis Health*, https://health.ucdavis.edu/what-you
    -can-do/facts.html, accessed February 12, 2021.

7. Resolution B007 of the 79th General Convention of The Episcopal
    Church, July 2018, https://www.episcopalarchives.org/cgi-bin/acts
    /acts_resolution.pl?resolution=2018-B007; see further, David Paulsen,
    "Episcopal Church Eyes Investing in Gun Manufacturers to Press for
    Greater Gun Safety," Episcopal News Service, https://www.episcopal
    newsservice.org/2018/12/14/episcopal-church-eyes-investing-in-gun
    -manufacturers-to-press-for-greater-gun-safety/, accessed September 1,
    2020.

8. This is the approach I preferred in my comments for the Episcopal News
    Service article above.

9. April Schentrup addressed Bishops United Against Gun Violence at
    the 79th General Convention of the Episcopal Church, Austin, TX,
    July 2018, https://bishopsagainstgunviolence.org/news_release/public
    -witness-at-gc79/, accessed March 1, 2021.